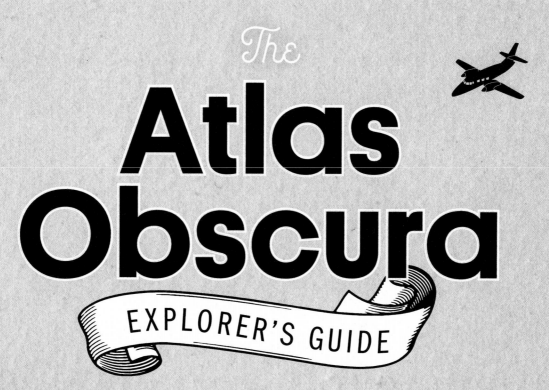

The Atlas Obscura

EXPLORER'S GUIDE

for

THE WORLD'S MOST ADVENTUROUS KID

Dylan Thuras and Rosemary Mosco

Illustrated by Joy Ang

WORKMAN PUBLISHING • NEW YORK

To Phineas and Jean, my two little human beans.
You are everything beautiful about the world.
—DYLAN THURAS

To my niece, who's just discovering this wonderful world.
And to my favorite fellow traveler—thank you for the
whale-filled, snake-filled, and lupine-filled adventures.
—ROSEMARY MOSCO

To an avid world traveler
and my supportive mom, Jonna.
—JOY ANG

Library of Congress Cataloging-in-Publication Data is available.
ISBN 978-1-5235-0354-4

Design by Janet Vicario and Sara Corbett
Editing by Danny Cooper
Production editing by Amanda Hong
Production management by Doug Wolff
Additional coloring by Ashley Mackenzie

Workman books are available at special discounts when purchased in bulk for
premiums and sales promotions as well as for fund-raising or educational use.
Special editions or book excerpts can also be created to specification. For details,
contact the Special Sales Director at the address below, or send an email
to specialmarkets@workman.com.

Workman Publishing Co., Inc.
225 Varick Street
New York, NY 10014-4381
workman.com

WORKMAN is a registered trademark
of Workman Publishing Co., Inc.
ATLAS OBSCURA is a registered trademark
of Atlas Obscura, Inc.

Printed in the United States of America
First printing August 2018

10 9 8 7 6 5 4 3 2 1

DEAR ADVENTURER,

We're about to tell you one of the greatest secrets of exploring. Are you ready? Here it is:

You are already somewhere amazing.

You may be on a farm. You may be in a small town or a big city. Perhaps you live in a desert, on a tropical island, or deep in a snowy forest. No matter where you are, you'll find surprises around hidden corners—or right below your feet.

Your world is crammed with wonders. But it's also curiously interconnected. Explore an ice cave in Argentina, then find another one—a little different, but just as amazing—across the ocean in Austria. Distant countries have more in common than you could ever imagine. You can travel halfway around the globe to see an incredible sight, then discover that there's something just like it *in your own neighborhood*.

This book is your passport to a world of hidden possibilities. You'll journey from lava lakes to dinosaur discos to forgotten underground cities, exploring the connections that bind your world together. As you travel, make sure to be respectful of the cultures and creatures you find. Tread lightly on the land. Be kind, curious, and ready to learn. The more we discover about each other, the better off we'll all be.

Every one of these places is absolutely real. But it's going to take you a long to time to see them all. You don't have a single moment to lose.

Are you ready? **Let's go.**

PACKING LIST

You're about to visit some of the world's most extreme places. You'll probably get cold. You'll certainly get hot. You'll zoom up mountains, drop down into caverns, and dive into the ocean. You can't prepare yourself for everything you're about to experience (that's part of the fun of traveling!), but here are some things you might want to pack.

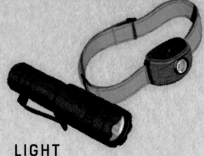

LIGHT

Pack a powerful flashlight. Also, bring a headlamp (a light that you strap onto your head for hands-free illumination).

SUN PROTECTION

Bring a hat, sunscreen, and anything else you need to cover up and avoid sunburn. Sunglasses are important, and in bright, snowy places, you'll need a powerful pair to cut the glare.

CAMERA

There are endless camera options, from the simple to the unusual. Here are some types to try:

- underwater
- infrared (to reveal the invisible light that you feel as heat)
- 3-D
- traditional film
- cell phone

Plus, bring along some interesting accessories. A macro lens, for instance, will let you photograph tiny insects as if they're huge monsters. A polarizing filter can cut through the glare on water surfaces to show what's below.

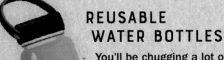

REUSABLE WATER BOTTLES

You'll be chugging a lot of water. For extra green points, carry reusable silverware and a straw, too!

OTHER OPTICS

You may want to carry binoculars or even a small telescope. You'll be heading to remote places where the light pollution is low and the sky is packed with stars.

THE RIGHT CLOTHES

Choosing clothes isn't just about fashion. It's a matter of life and death. Cotton soaks up moisture, and you don't want to be cold and wet—you risk a dangerous drop in body temperature called hypothermia. So ditch the jeans. Wool and some synthetic materials will keep you dry, and they'll save your feet from stinking on day 15.

BOOKS

These will keep you from getting bored on long plane, car, train, and boat rides. Try puzzle books, travel guides, or long, exciting fantasy stories.

REPAIR KIT

A needle, some thread, and duct tape: These will help you fix broken stuff—and maybe get you out of a jam or two.

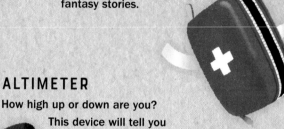

FIRST AID KIT

Hopefully you won't need this, but it's smart to be prepared!

ALTIMETER

How high up or down are you? This device will tell you your precise altitude.

GEIGER COUNTER

Use it to detect harmful radioactive stuff.

ART SUPPLIES

Sometimes the best way to capture the sights you see—and the emotions you feel while you see them—is to make art. Bring watercolors, colored pencils, or any other (portable) supplies you love to use.

SATELLITE PHONE

It'll work anywhere . . . even in the desert or the middle of the ocean!

TOWEL

It's about the most massively useful thing a globe-trotting kid can have.

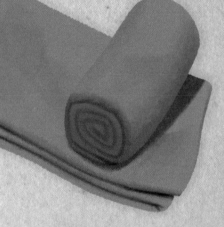

SOLAR CHARGER

Charge your phone and any other electronics with the power of the sun.

GOAT TREATS

Just in case you run into some adorable, hungry goats . . .

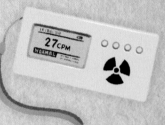

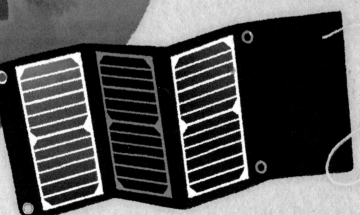

ADVENTURE PLAN

★ On each page, next to the name of the city, town, or region, you'll find a set of numbers and letters that look like this: Ⓝ 60.9025 Ⓔ 101.9045. These are your destination's *latitude* and *longitude*. What do they mean? They're a kind of special code. Picture a huge grid of lines crisscrossing the surface of the Earth. Lines of latitude stretch from east to west, and lines of longitude run from the North Pole to the South Pole. The numbers and letters give you the exact coordinates of your destination on this grid. Here's the coolest part: If you type the coordinates into Google Maps (or another online map service), it'll take you right there!

ICELAND

Thrihnukagigur

Húsavík

LOCATION: northern Atlantic Ocean

POPULATION: 332,529—just a third of Rhode Island's

CAPITAL: Reykjavík, the world's northernmost national capital

OBSCURE FACT: Iceland has the world's only school dedicated to the study of elves.

Volcanic Vistas

Inside Thrihnukagigur Volcano

Hafnarfjörður, Capital Region Ⓝ 63.9985 Ⓦ 21.6990

What does the inside of a volcano look like? Why not see for yourself? Strap on a helmet and a harness, step into an open elevator car, and drop down into the rocky heart of Thrihnukagigur Volcano.

Don't worry—you won't burn to a crisp. Yes, you're entering an enormous chamber that once held magma, but it's now empty. Thrihnukagigur hasn't erupted for more than 4,000 years.

As your elevator car slowly descends, you'll notice two things. First, this space is big. The Statue of Liberty could fit inside it with room to spare. But here's what'll really take your breath away: The walls glitter with a rainbow of minerals. By the light of your headlamp, you'll see purples blending into dazzling oranges and yellows. Fingers of cooled, hardened magma drip down the walls.

Who knew there were such wonders below your feet? Oh, but you're just getting started . . .

Massive Migrations

Blue Whale Migration Near Húsavík

Norðurþing, Northeastern Region Ⓝ 66.0450 Ⓦ 17.3383

As you steady yourself on the rocking deck of a ship, you hear a sound like a cannon blast. The largest animal on the planet has surfaced beside you. Its blow rises almost as high as a 3-story building. Its blue body, longer than two city buses, makes your boat seem like a toy.

Blue whales are heftier than the biggest dinosaurs. Yet they're sleek travelers. When they're in a hurry, they zoom along at 30 miles per hour (48.3 kph). Every year, they migrate between warmer waters (where they give birth) and colder seas near the poles (where there's food). In May and June, some hang out here in the bay north of Húsavík.

Every sighting is special—and rare. Because of past hunting, there aren't many blue whales left in the world. Perhaps a thousand swim in the North Atlantic. But almost one in five has stopped by this Icelandic bay, so it's a smart choice for an unforgettable encounter.

Experience another amazing migration 5,947 miles (9,571 km) away. If you rode a blue whale, it'd take you more than eight days to get there at top speed . . . and you'd have to dig some canals.

ZAMBIA

LOCATION: southern Africa, surrounded by eight countries

NAME: from Zambezi, one of Africa's longest rivers

FOOD: Nshima is a cornmeal dish that Zambians eat with relishes made of meat, beans, or veggies.

OBSCURE FACT: Zambia declared independence during the 1964 Tokyo Olympics, becoming the first nation to enter and leave the games as different countries.

Fruit Bats

Devil's Swimming Pool

Massive Migrations

Fruit Bats of Kasanka National Park

Serenje District, Central Province Ⓢ 12.5833 Ⓔ 30.2000

As the sun sets over the forest in Kasanka National Park, you'll witness one of Africa's biggest, most surprising animal phenomena. Ten million shrieking bats leave their treetop roosts and fill the skies. That's more than half the number of people in all of Zambia! The bats are big, about the size of crows, with wingspans as wide as 3 feet (0.9 m). And they're hungry.

Fortunately, you're not on the menu. These are fruit bats—straw-colored fruit bats, to be precise—and they've migrated here to eat the forest's ripe fruits. They spend the night gorging and napping. At dawn, they take to the skies again, returning to their roosting trees.

The bats hang out at Kasanka only between October and December. Once they've scarfed down all the fruit, they fly off, leaving behind a forest stripped bare.

Wild Waterfalls

Devil's Swimming Pool

Livingstone, Southern Province ⓈS 17.9244 ⓔE 25.8568

Paddle to the edge of this natural pool and look down. What you see will make your heart pound. The Devil's Swimming Pool sits right at the lip of an enormous waterfall. From here, Victoria Falls plunges 355 feet (108 m) down. It's taller than London's Big Ben clock tower.

Why doesn't the force of the rushing water carry you over the edge? Surprisingly, there's not much current in the pool itself. Hidden below the surface is a barrier of rock that separates it from the surrounding falls. You can swim in the pool only during the dry season—from about September to November—when the water level is just right. If you entered it at any other time of year, you'd be washed over the edge to a watery doom.

Antarctica has an even weirder waterfall. There are just a couple of ways to see it: Head to McMurdo Station or Scott Base and hop on a helicopter, or take a Ross Sea cruise.

ANTARCTICA

Blood Falls

Mount Erebus

LOCATION: the southernmost part of the world

POPULATION: 4,000 in summer, 1,000 in winter

AREA: 5.4 million square miles (14 million km^2); larger than Canada (but smaller than Russia)

OBSCURE FACT: Its largest native land animal is an insect— a flightless midge, only about 0.1 inch (3 mm) long.

Wild Waterfalls

Blood Falls

McMurdo Dry Valleys, Victoria Land Ⓢ **77.7167** Ⓔ **162.2668**

Antarctica is a stark, mostly colorless place. Gray, rocky peaks jut up from icy plains. But at the foot of one special glacier, you'll find a five-story-tall red waterfall gushing from the ice like blood from a wound. Welcome to Blood Falls.

It's a gory sight, but that liquid isn't really blood. It's something *much weirder*. Two million years ago, an ice sheet called Taylor Glacier flowed over a lake, covering it like a lid on a pot and sealing it away. As the glacier scraped at the bedrock and bacteria munched the rock, little bits of iron entered the lake water. Today, some of that iron-rich fluid leaks through a crack in the glacier and cascades out. When it hits the air, the iron rusts— so the water turns red!

The lake below Taylor Glacier is also home to a lost world of microscopic creatures. By studying them, we can learn how alien life might thrive on icy planets far, far away.

Lava Lakes

Mount Erebus

Ross Island Ⓢ 77.5274 Ⓔ 167.1567

Towering above the frigid Antarctic landscape, Mount Erebus has a hot secret. The southernmost active volcano on Earth, it's home to a lake of boiling, gurgling lava.

Erebus was named after the Greek god of darkness, who was the son of Chaos. It's a fitting name. During the sunless Antarctic winter, the temperature at Erebus averages –50°F (–46°C). You should climb it during the summer, when temperatures average a not-so-balmy –4°F (–20°C). Even so, cover up with high-tech, heavily insulated ECW (Extreme Cold Weather) gear, or you'll become a human-shaped ice cube.

As you climb, you'll find a few places that are a little less chilly. Hot gases hiss out of the volcano's core and carve caves of blue ice full of glittering frost crystals.

At the summit, you'll gaze down at the mountain's fiery heart. It's a lake of bright lava that reaches a scorching 1,700°F (927°C), hot enough to melt brass. Watch out: Chaotic Erebus sometimes belches out volcanic bombs—lava chunks the size of small cars!

There are only six known lava lakes in the world. Journey across the Antarctic and Indian Oceans to Ethiopia, where

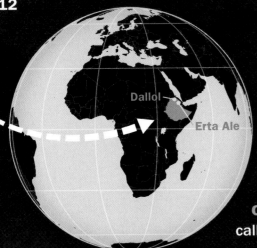

Dallol

Erta Ale

ETHIOPIA

LOCATION: northeast Africa, on a peninsula called the Horn of Africa

NATIONAL ANIMAL: lion

CALENDAR: 13 months per year, with 12 months lasting 30 days and an extra 5- or 6-day month

OBSCURE FACT: On August 19, kids celebrate a Halloween-like holiday called Buhe, going door-to-door asking for bread and money.

Lava Lakes

Erta Ale

Afar, Afar Triangle Ⓝ 13.6460 Ⓔ 40.6805

Welcome to a place so fierce it's known as "Hell on Earth." Daytime temperatures can climb higher than 120°F (49°C). Only 4 to 8 inches (100–200 mm) of rainfall per year wet the parched landscape. And that's not all—here, the Earth's crust is tearing itself apart.

Millions of years from now, this region will split open wide enough that a whole new sea will fill it. For now, you get to witness the ocean's slow, violent birth. Geysers of boiling water spray into the sky. Hot springs simmer. Volcanoes dot the landscape.

When you reach the volcanic mountain of Erta Ale, there's a good chance you'll see not one but two lakes of bubbling lava. These rare pools form only under special conditions. When lava is heated just right, it never solidifies for long and circulates continually like water in a boiling pot. When the sun goes down, these exceptional lakes glow like hot coals in the darkness.

Weather Extremes

Dallol, Hottest Place

Dallol, Afar Triangle Ⓝ 14.2417 Ⓔ 40.3000

Do you like warm weather or cool weather? Maybe you enjoy inhaling the frosty air on a cold winter morning and feeling your nose hairs freeze. But if you prefer things hot—really, *really* hot—you'll adore Dallol. It sits at a very low elevation and gets tons of sunlight from directly overhead. Plus, there's almost no rain. With an average temperature of 94°F (34°C), it's one of the toastiest places on Earth.

Believe it or not, people lived and worked in Dallol decades ago. You'll find abandoned buildings that once housed miners. They worked to dig up a substance called potash, a plant fertilizer. Since the extreme conditions would damage many building materials, the houses were made of salt blocks.

Be sure to steer your jeep past Dallol's incredibly colorful hot springs. Neon-yellow and orange minerals surround emerald-green pools. It's like visiting another planet. You won't need a space suit, but you should definitely bring a *lot* of water.

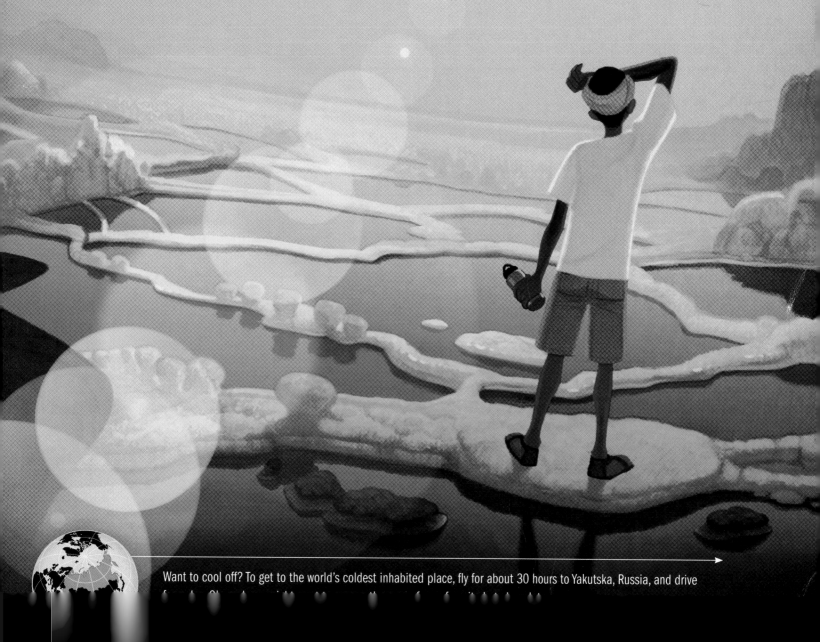

Want to cool off? To get to the world's coldest inhabited place, fly for about 30 hours to Yakutska, Russia, and drive

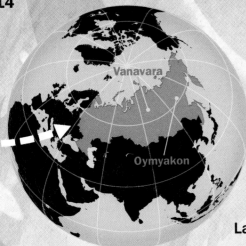

RUSSIA

LOCATION: eastern Europe and northern Asia

AREA: the world's largest country, at 6.6 million square miles (17 million km²)

TIME: Russia spans 11 time zones.

OBSCURE FACT: The largest freshwater lake in the world, Lake Baikal, holds one fifth of the world's fresh surface water.

Weather Extremes

Oymyakon, Coldest Inhabited Place

Oymyakon, Sakha Republic Ⓝ 63.4641 Ⓔ 142.7737

The kids of Oymyakon, the coldest town on Earth, are tough. Really tough. They're so used to harsh weather that their school doesn't close unless the temperature drops below –61.6°F (–52°C).

Oymyakon gets this cold because it's just a few hundred miles from the Arctic Circle. In winter, nighttime temperatures plummet to –60°F (–51°C). It's so cold that many things we take for granted just don't work. Electronic devices freeze up. Cars won't start unless their garages are heated. The ground is frozen, so few veggies can grow. When someone dies and the townspeople want to bury the body, they light a bonfire and wait for the ground to thaw so they can dig a grave!

In the summertime, though, the living is a little easier. Temperatures rise to a comfortable 70°F (21°C). Some days, there are 21 straight hours of sunlight. That's a lot of time for outdoor sports— or long rides on a Yakutian horse, the local breed of shaggy, cold-tolerant steed.

Explosions from Space
The Tunguska Event
Vanavara, Krasnoyarsk Krai Ⓝ 60.9025 Ⓔ 101.9045

Early one morning in June 1908, Siberian villagers saw a bright light streak across the sky. A moment later, their world was turned upside down. A massive blast knocked people out of their chairs. Windows shattered. Eighty million trees toppled over. Shock waves rippled all the way to Europe.

The Tunguska Event was an explosion many times larger than the atomic bombing of Hiroshima. But no country had fired a weapon into the Siberian woods, and for a long time, the cause of the event was a mystery. Though the event flattened the forest, somehow there was no impact crater.

Can you guess what happened?

In the past, some people blamed UFOs or secret experiments. Most scientists now think the real cause was a meteorite or comet. When this chunk of rock or ice slammed into Earth's atmosphere, it exploded in the sky. Today, you can still see gnarled trees that were knocked over by the blast.

Journey on to the site of the most famous space impact: the one that killed almost all the dinosaurs. It's 6,725 miles (10,823 km) away as the crow (a modern-day dino) flies.

MEXICO

LOCATION: southern North America

LANGUAGE: Some English words come from Mexico's Aztec language, like "chocolate" and "tomato."

COAT OF ARMS: an eagle on a cactus eating a rattlesnake

OBSCURE FACT: In 1943, a volcano burst up from a farmer's field in the state of Michoacán. For the first time, scientists were able to study a volcano from its birth to its death.

Chicxulub

Naica

Explosions from Space
Chicxulub Crater
Chicxulub, Yucatán Ⓝ 21.2777 Ⓦ 89.5012

It was a typical day in the Cretaceous period, 65 million years ago. A herd of plant-eating dinosaurs lowered their enormous heads to munch on some tasty vegetation. Suddenly, a bright light flashed in the sky. The dinos blinked. Then everything changed.

A massive space rock slammed into Earth. The force of the impact was more than five million times stronger than the most powerful bomb. The air baked and wildfires raged. Soot rose and blocked the sun's rays. When the dust settled, three out of every four species on Earth were gone.

You can visit the impact crater on Mexico's Yucatán Peninsula. It's named after a small town called Chicxulub. As you drive into Chicxulub, you'll find a monument to those departed dinos, but you won't see the crater. That's because it's so wide—a whopping 110 miles (177 km) across. But look for Mexico's many colorful bird species. Birds are the only living descendants of the dinos.

Incredible Caves

Giant Crystals of Naica

Naica, Chihuahua Ⓝ 27.8508 Ⓦ 105.4964

In 2000, workers at a Mexican mine were excavating a new tunnel when they stumbled across a cave of glittering crystals. These weren't the small gems you might see in a necklace or ring. They were seven times taller than a person. Some of them weighed as much as ten elephants.

The huge crystals at Naica are made of a mineral called selenite. Crystals can only grow this big when they're kept in stable conditions over a very long period of time. In this case, the cave was bathed in mineral-rich water at a constant temperature of 136°F (58°C) for half a million years.

What's good for the formation of giant crystals isn't so good for human explorers. The air hits a scorching 125°F (52°C), and it's thick with moisture. Sharp crystal shards litter the ground. You'll need to wear a special suit lined with ice, and even with the proper equipment, you should head back to the surface after just 30 or 45 minutes.

If you like spelunking underground, go to Southeast Asia and join a trek to the world's largest cave that's open to exploration. You'll hike through the jungle and use ropes to climb into this cave!

VIETNAM

Hang Son Doong

Ho Thuy Tien

LOCATION: southeast Asia along the South China Sea

CULTURE: Tet, or New Year's, the country's biggest celebration, occurs in January or February.

FOOD: pho, a comforting soup with rice noodles, meat, and herbs

OBSCURE FACT: Vietnamese people have a long tradition of water puppetry—puppet shows that take place on water.

Incredible Caves
Hang Son Doong

Phong Nha-Ke Bang, Quang Bình Province
Ⓝ 17.5431 Ⓔ 106.1448

Welcome to the world's largest cave. Its biggest chamber is more than 3 miles (4.8 km) long. Its ceiling is higher than the Great Pyramid of Giza, and you could fly a 747 airplane through it.

The cave of Hang Son Doong sits inside a lush preserve called Phong Nha-Ke Bang National Park. The forest is full of deep mysteries. Underground rivers, including one of the world's longest, bubble in the shadows. Scientists are still finding new species here. One large mammal, the gazelle-like saola, or "Asian unicorn," hid from discovery until 1992. And Hang Son Doong itself remained hidden until 1991, when a local farmer ducked inside during a rainstorm—and was shocked to find that his shelter was a little bigger than he'd expected.

(Psst: Locals recently claimed to have discovered an even larger cave, but they're keeping its location a secret. For now, Hang Son Doong is the biggest cave you can visit.)

Abandoned Amusement Parks

Ho Thuy Tien Water Park

Ho Thuy Tien, Thua Thien–Hue Province
Ⓝ 16.41136 Ⓔ 107.5760

The water park of Ho Thuy Tien was an expensive disaster. It cost $3 million to build. Only a few years after it opened in 2004, business problems forced it to close. But that wasn't the end of the story. Now that the water park has officially shut down, it's more popular than ever.

Adventurers come from around the world to marvel at the collapsing park. They love it because it's weird, spooky, and beautiful. Its buildings are crumbling and the jungle is slowly taking over. Huge, broken water slides peek out from the trees. A 3-story-tall metal dragon scowls above an empty aquarium. At one time, hungry escaped crocodiles roamed the park. Luckily, they've all been captured and taken to a preserve.

Ho Thuy Tien is so attractive to tourists that the locals have started charging admission and selling drinks and snacks. It's almost like a real amusement park! Just don't go on any of the slides. . . .

Fly northwest across Asia to explore another of the world's strangest abandoned theme parks, in Ukraine. You'll need

UKRAINE

LOCATION: eastern Europe, north of the Black Sea

AREA: 233,062 square miles (603,648 km²), the largest country in Europe (after Russia)

GEOGRAPHICAL FEATURE: Thanks to its fertile black soil, 70 percent of the land is used for agriculture.

OBSCURE FACT: The Pysanka Museum celebrates Ukraine's special dyed Easter eggs covered in intricate patterns.

Abandoned Amusement Parks

Pripyat

Pripyat, Kiev Oblast Ⓝ 51.4056 Ⓔ 30.0569

The city of Pripyat was founded in 1970. Just 16 years later, everyone left it in a hurry. Today, you're only allowed to visit if you follow some specific rules. Be sure to cover up your arms, legs, and feet. Oh, and *don't touch anything*.

What happened to Pripyat? This town was built for people who worked at the nearby Chernobyl nuclear power station. On April 26, 1986, the station exploded, launching dangerous radioactive particles into the sky—particles that could make people sick with cancer and other illnesses.

The citizens of Pripyat fled the city as quickly as possible. They left behind many things, including amusement park rides set up for a May Day carnival. These days, you can still see a Ferris wheel and bumper cars, but they're rusting away. The forest is slowly taking over. Lynx, moose, wolves, and other wildlife now prowl the ruins.

Creepy Catacombs

Odessa Catacombs

Odessa, Odessa Oblast Ⓝ 46.5467 Ⓔ 30.6306

Beneath one of Ukraine's largest cities, you'll find a maze of dark, creepy passageways. The Odessa Catacombs are truly enormous—at about 1,500 miles (2,414 km), they're more than six times as long as all the routes of the New York City subway combined.

Who built and used these spooky tunnels? Miners created the largest section in the 1800s as they excavated limestone for building material. During World War II, Ukrainian rebel groups hid out in the catacombs and launched sneak attacks on enemy German soldiers. After the war, smugglers and other criminals took over, adding their own passages. These days, teams of explorers work to map out the whole system. They sometimes discover old weapons—and even the skeletons of long-dead soldiers.

You can experience part of the catacombs at the Museum of Partisan Glory in Nerubayskoye, northwest of Odessa. You'll also see weapons and other artifacts that explorers have uncovered during their long treks through the shadowy tunnels.

ITALY

LOCATION: southern Europe, on the Mediterranean Sea

HISTORY: The ancient Roman Empire once covered about 5 million square miles (13 million km²), 43 times the size of modern Italy.

GEOGRAPHICAL FEATURE: The longest river has a short name: Po.

OBSCURE FACT: Hundreds of cats find sanctuary at the ancient ruins Largo di Torre Argentina, where Julius Caesar was assassinated.

Creepy Catacombs

Capuchin Catacombs

Palermo, Sicily Ⓝ 38.1118 Ⓔ 13.3392

From the outside, the Capuchin monastery in Palermo is a simple beige building. Head in and walk down to the limestone basement, and you'll be face-to-face with corpses. *Eight thousand* corpses.

The empty eye sockets of monks stare back at you. They're wearing funeral clothes, and many still have skin. The oldest is a friar who died in 1599. You'll also find bodies of wealthy people who paid to have themselves—and their family members—interred here. They include doctors, judges, and artists. The youngest is a two-year-old girl who died of pneumonia in 1920.

These days, no new "residents" are added to the catacombs. But the dry atmosphere will help to preserve the bodies for a long time to come. It's a creepy but peaceful final resting place for the Capuchin monks and their neighbors.

Cliff Dwellings

Pitigliano

Pitigliano, Tuscany Ⓝ 42.6353 Ⓔ 11.6700

Would you rather live deep underground or high in the sky? Maybe you'd prefer a high-rise apartment so you can enjoy an amazing view and feel like you're above it all. Back before skyscrapers existed, some people did the next best thing: They built their houses right on cliffs.

The town of Pitigliano is a cliff-top paradise. It sits on a towering outcrop of rock called tuff that's made of ash from ancient volcanic eruptions. The centuries-old buildings reach right to the edge of the cliffs and almost look like they sprouted out of them.

Inside Pitigliano you'll find narrow cobblestone streets and twisting stairs. There's a lot to experience, from mouthwatering local cheeses and sausages to a big spring festival complete with a burning wooden figure to symbolize the end of winter. Just don't forget to stop at lookout point Piazza Becherini to enjoy the view of the vineyards and valleys below.

Love heights? Check out Datong, China, for more cliff-side architecture. Here's a tip: Take a side trip to see the nearby Yungang Grottoes, a set of caves containing 51,000 statues of Buddha and other figures.

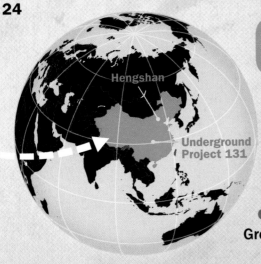

Hengshan

Underground
Project 131

CHINA

LOCATION: eastern Asia

POPULATION: 1.4 billion, more than any other country

HISTORY: birthplace of many famous philosophers, including Confucius and Lao-tzu

OBSCURE FACT: Sticky rice was added to the mortar in the Great Wall to help glue it together.

Cliff Dwellings

Hanging Temple of Hengshan

Mount Heng, Shanxi Ⓝ 39.6739 Ⓔ 113.7356

According to legend, an especially daring monk named Liao Ran built this temple on a sheer rocky cliff more than 1,400 years ago. The Hanging Temple of Hengshan perches a dizzying 246 feet (75 m) above the ground—about the height of a 22-story building. Why doesn't it fall down? Huge wooden poles, set into holes drilled right into the cliff, hold up the structure.

This may seem like a dangerous place for a temple. But the unique location has helped to preserve it through the centuries. The rock keeps it protected from wind, snow, and sun damage.

The Hanging Temple of Hengshan is special for another reason. Uniquely, it mixes design elements from Confucianism, Taoism, and Buddhism in 78 statues and carvings. Look closely and you'll spot hidden details in the architecture, from grinning faces to roaring beasts. Just be careful on the narrow, packed stairways. And if you hate heights, well, *don't look down.*

Forgotten Subterranean Worlds

Underground Project 131

Gaoqiao, Hubei Ⓝ **31.2218** Ⓔ **110.5526**

In the 1960s, China's leader, Mao Tse-tung, was worried about the threat of nuclear war. How could he protect people from bombs that could destroy *whole cities*? The solution, he decided, was to bring those cities underground.

Mao ordered the construction of subterranean towns where people could hide if war broke out. Underground Project 131 was one such space. Even though it was basically a damp, sunless basement, it was designed to give its citizens the most comfortable lives possible. It had schools, stores, restaurants, and more.

Underground Project 131 was also going to be the headquarters of the Chinese military. It would be a place where Mao could hide out and command his troops. But political squabbling put an end to construction before the city was completed. Today, it has a fancy hotel and a garden aboveground—and many eerily empty rooms below.

It's 7,670 miles (12,344 km) to another underground world: an abandoned science center. Fly to Dallas, Texas, and gallop south on the back of an American Quarter Horse, the state horse of Texas. The center is near the Wagon Wheel Cowboy Church.

TEXAS

LOCATION: south-central United States, along the Gulf of Mexico

AREA: 268,581 square miles (695,622 km²), the second largest state (after Alaska)

STATE REPTILE: Texas horned lizard

OBSCURE FACT: The town of Paris, Texas, has its own Eiffel Tower—with a red cowboy hat on top.

10,000-Year Clock

Super Collider

Forgotten Subterranean Worlds
Superconducting Super Collider
Waxahachie Ⓝ 32.3865 Ⓦ 96.8483

In the 1990s, construction began on a truly amazing science lab, nicknamed the "Desertron." The plans called for an underground ring-shaped tunnel more than 54 miles (87 km) in circumference. Scientists would send streams of tiny particles through it and smash them together with record-breaking energy. These experiments would help them discover the smallest building blocks of the universe.

Unfortunately, as construction went on, the project started costing way more than expected. The US Congress shut it down after only 14 miles (23 km) of tunnel were excavated. It's a real shame, because scientists at its European counterpart, the Large Hadron Collider, have been discovering all sorts of fascinating new particles.

So what do you do with 14 miles of abandoned tunnel in the middle of North Texas? Create an amazing skateboarding park? People have proposed all sorts of uses for it, including data storage or a mushroom farm. Nowadays, a chemical company owns it. They're probably not skateboarding in it . . . *probably*.

Planning for the Future

10,000-Year Clock

Van Horn Ⓝ **31.0399** Ⓦ **104.8308**

Think about the appliances in your home: your fridge, toaster, or TV. How long will they keep working before they break? Some will fail after just a few months of use. But what if they were designed to last for hundreds—even thousands—of years?

Deep inside a west Texas mountain there's an enormous clock that will run for a whopping 10,000 years. Two hundred feet (61 m) tall, with gears 8 feet (2.4 m) wide, it's powered by energy created when the mountain heats up during the day. The project's creators hope that it will help people think beyond today and focus on our future.

To visit it, you'll have to hike for hours through the desert. Find a jade door that opens into a pitch-black tunnel. Then climb a spiral staircase cut from stone. At the top you can wind the clock to hear a chiming song just for you. The chimes will never repeat the same tune in all those 10,000 years.

Want to keep thinking long-term? Hike out of the desert, fly into Oslo, and head for the cool Norwegian woods of Nordmarka to view a futuristic art project.

NORWAY

LOCATION: northern Europe on the Scandinavian Peninsula

GEOGRAPHICAL FEATURE: rugged coastline with 50,000 islands

LANGUAGE: Norwegian, a descendant of Old Norse

OBSCURE FACT: You may see a goat-shaped decoration on Christmas trees; that's the *julebukk*, or Yule goat, who brings gifts to Norwegian children.

Planning for the Future

Forest of the Future Library

Nordmarka, Oslomarka Ⓝ 59.9863 Ⓔ 10.6969

In 2014, artist Katie Paterson began work on a *very* long-term art project. She planted 1,000 baby spruce trees in the Norwegian wilderness of Nordmarka. In 100 years, when the trees are fully grown, they'll be cut down to make paper for a remarkable set of books.

Paterson's project is called the Future Library. Famous authors are writing books for it, and they won't let anyone read their creations . . . until the year 2114. That's when the spruce forest will be turned into books printed with the stories for all to enjoy. Would you be able to wait an entire century for a book from your favorite author?

For many of us, it's easier to make quick, short-term decisions (should you eat that candy bar?), but much harder to plan for the future (are you saving enough for that fancy bike you want?). With her project, Paterson hopes to make you think past today's flashy distractions.

Saving Seed

Svalbard Global Seed Vault

Longyearbyen, Svalbard Ⓝ 78.2382 Ⓔ 15.4472

The Norwegian island of Spitsbergen is a cold, barren place. Polar bears and reindeer roam the icy wastes. But down in a high-security vault kept at –0.4°F (–18°C), you'll find the seeds of a lush, green world.

The Svalbard seed bank was built to hold millions of seeds from veggies, wheat, and other agricultural plants. Why create a bank for seeds? Most of the plants we eat are clones of each other—they have the same genes. That's good because it means they all taste and look similar. But it's bad because they get sick in the same way. If one plant caught a nasty disease, all of them could die.

Enter the Svalbard Global Seed Vault. It keeps a wide variety of samples, including rare strains, safe in a freezing cold vault. Thousands of years from now, they'll still be able to sprout, bringing new life and new genes to farmers' fields.

To see more special seeds, cross 2,920 miles (4,700 km) to Kazakhstan and head to Ile-Alatau National Park, also

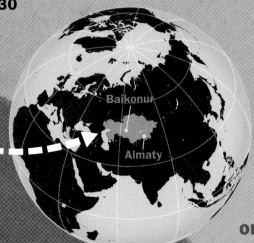

KAZAKHSTAN

LOCATION: central Asia, south of Russia

NAME: a blend of Turkic and Persian words meaning "Land of Wanderers"

AREA: 1,052,100 square miles (2,724,926 km²), the largest former Soviet Socialist republic after Russia

OBSCURE FACT: You can skate in a mountain valley at Medeu, the highest ice rink in the world at 5,548 feet (1,691 m).

Saving Seed

The Last Wild Apple Forests

Almaty N 43.2220 E 76.8512

Next time you bite into a crunchy apple, take a moment to think about where your snack came from. That fruit ripened in a farmer's orchard—but where? These days, apples grow all over the world, from Brazil to Poland to Japan. But some of the key ancestors of all apple trees came from a very special place: the mountains around Almaty, the largest city in Kazakhstan and the "fatherland of apples."

Here, you can still find wild apple forests growing in patches among the hills. The trees grow wild and tangled. Their fruit comes in all sorts of sizes, colors, and even flavors, from honey to licorice. Many of these forests have been cut down to make room for farms and homes. But scientists and apple lovers are working hard to protect the remaining trees. Their precious seeds could help us develop better, tastier apples.

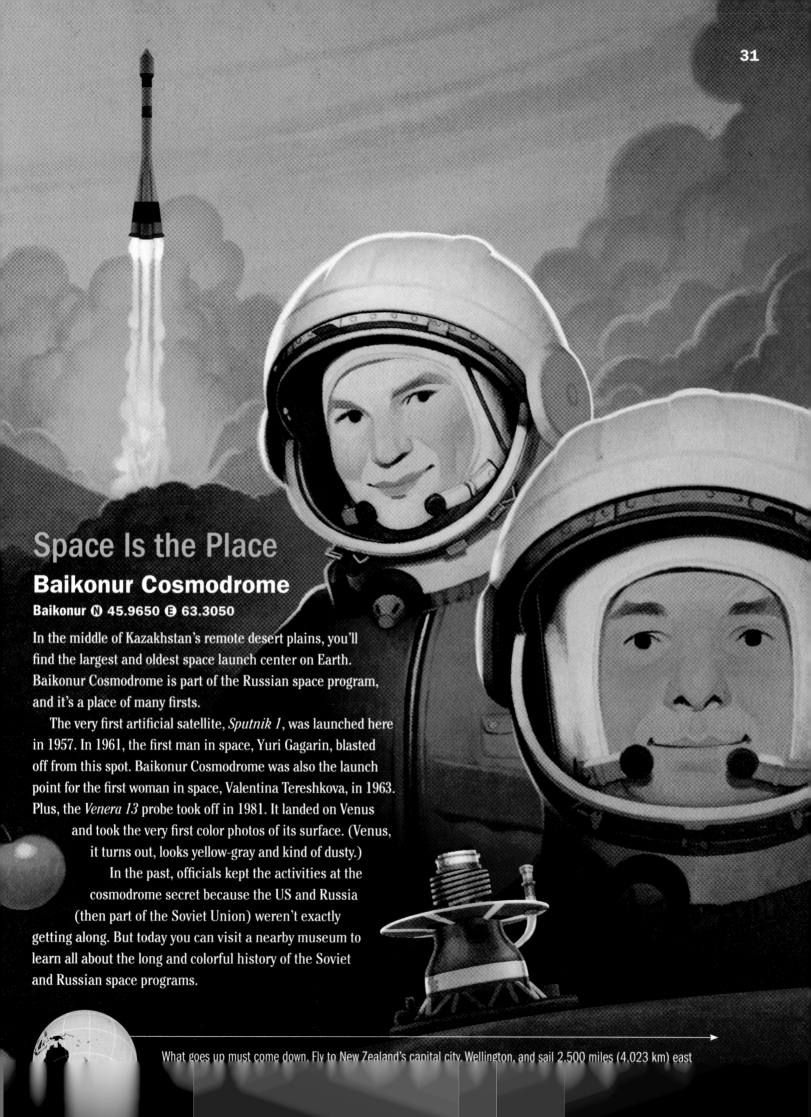

Space Is the Place

Baikonur Cosmodrome

Baikonur Ⓝ 45.9650 Ⓔ 63.3050

In the middle of Kazakhstan's remote desert plains, you'll find the largest and oldest space launch center on Earth. Baikonur Cosmodrome is part of the Russian space program, and it's a place of many firsts.

The very first artificial satellite, *Sputnik 1*, was launched here in 1957. In 1961, the first man in space, Yuri Gagarin, blasted off from this spot. Baikonur Cosmodrome was also the launch point for the first woman in space, Valentina Tereshkova, in 1963. Plus, the *Venera 13* probe took off in 1981. It landed on Venus and took the very first color photos of its surface. (Venus, it turns out, looks yellow-gray and kind of dusty.) In the past, officials kept the activities at the cosmodrome secret because the US and Russia (then part of the Soviet Union) weren't exactly getting along. But today you can visit a nearby museum to learn all about the long and colorful history of the Soviet and Russian space programs.

What goes up must come down. Fly to New Zealand's capital city, Wellington, and sail 2,500 miles (4,023 km) east

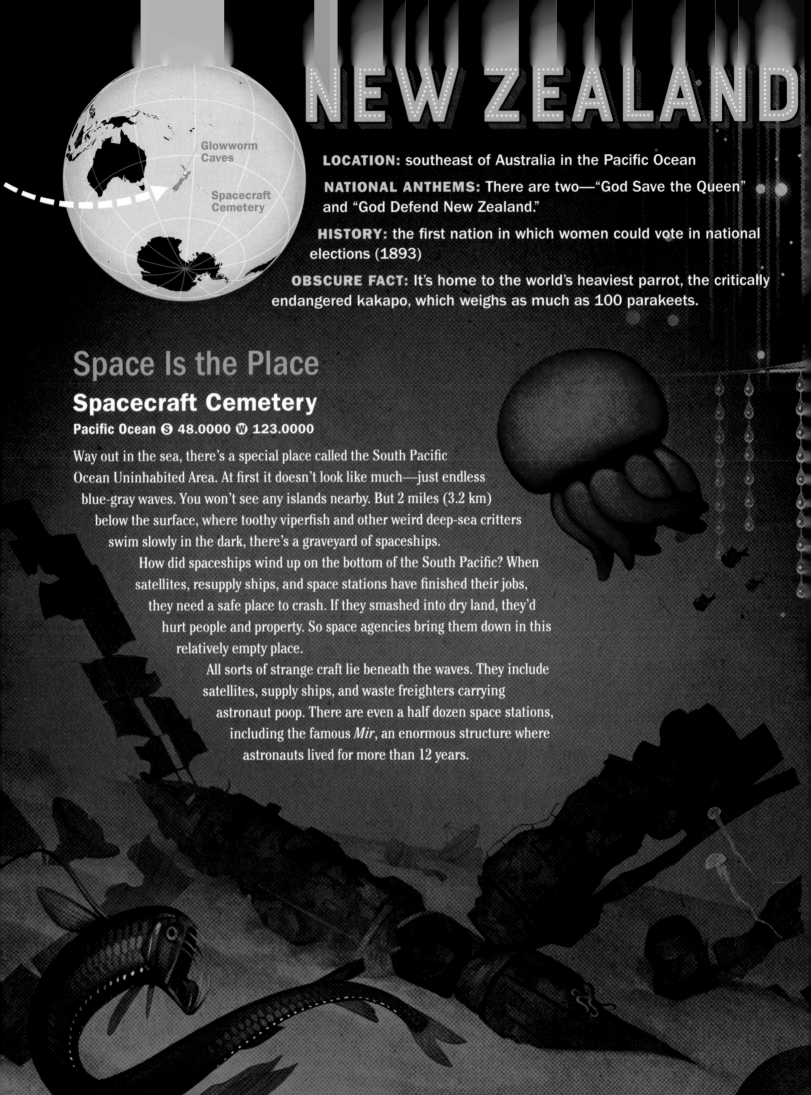

NEW ZEALAND

LOCATION: southeast of Australia in the Pacific Ocean

NATIONAL ANTHEMS: There are two—"God Save the Queen" and "God Defend New Zealand."

HISTORY: the first nation in which women could vote in national elections (1893)

OBSCURE FACT: It's home to the world's heaviest parrot, the critically endangered kakapo, which weighs as much as 100 parakeets.

Glowworm Caves

Spacecraft Cemetery

Space Is the Place

Spacecraft Cemetery
Pacific Ocean Ⓢ 48.0000 Ⓦ 123.0000

Way out in the sea, there's a special place called the South Pacific Ocean Uninhabited Area. At first it doesn't look like much—just endless blue-gray waves. You won't see any islands nearby. But 2 miles (3.2 km) below the surface, where toothy viperfish and other weird deep-sea critters swim slowly in the dark, there's a graveyard of spaceships.

How did spaceships wind up on the bottom of the South Pacific? When satellites, resupply ships, and space stations have finished their jobs, they need a safe place to crash. If they smashed into dry land, they'd hurt people and property. So space agencies bring them down in this relatively empty place.

All sorts of strange craft lie beneath the waves. They include satellites, supply ships, and waste freighters carrying astronaut poop. There are even a half dozen space stations, including the famous *Mir*, an enormous structure where astronauts lived for more than 12 years.

Bioluminescent Beasts
Waitomo Glowworm Caves
Waitomo, Waikato ⑤ 38.2510 ⓔ 175.1710

In 1887, a Maori chief called Tane Tinorau and an English surveyor named Fred Mace entered a series of mysterious caves. They launched a raft into an underground stream and paddled along in the darkness. Soon they saw a strange glow. A galaxy of blue-green stars glittered on the cave's ceiling.

This underground starlight comes from glowworms. They aren't really worms, but gnats (a type of fly), and they create light through chemical reactions called *bioluminescence*. Glowworms use their lights—which just happen to be on their butts—to "fish" for dinner. They perch on the cave ceiling and dangle sticky silken threads. Tasty insects are drawn to the lights and get stuck.

You can take your own paddling adventure through the Waitomo caves. You're not allowed to take pictures, but that's okay. You'll never forget the sight of that underground galaxy.

Cross the Pacific to the United States, catch a ride into the Tennessee hills, and meet some of the most beguiling bioluminescent beasts. Time your trip carefully: They shine for only two weeks in May or June.

TENNESSEE

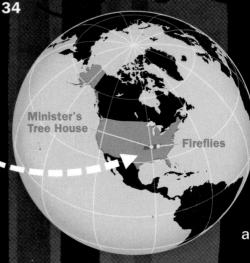

Minister's Tree House

Fireflies

LOCATION: southeastern United States

STATE AMPHIBIAN: Tennessee cave salamander

GEOGRAPHICAL FEATURE: the Lost Sea, the largest underground lake in the US

OBSCURE FACT: Tennessee has tons of quirky museums, including a teapot museum and a salt-and-pepper-shaker museum.

Bioluminescent Beasts

Fireflies of the Great Smoky Mountains

Elkmont ⓝ 35.6856 ⓦ 83.5366

The synchronous fireflies of Tennessee's Great Smoky Mountains are a little different from the ones you'll see in your backyard. They gather by the thousands in a dark forest and blink their lights at *exactly the same time*, like a big flashing neon sign.

These fireflies are famous around the world for their astonishing light show. But they spend most of their lives far from the spotlight. As larvae, they crawl around in the darkness underground and eat smaller critters like worms. After a year or two, they become adults. Then it's showtime! For just a few short weeks the males put on their best possible light display, hoping to attract a mate. By flashing in synch, they may make their signal brighter and clearer for females.

That's when their popularity soars. In fact, you'll need to enter a lottery for a chance to see them. With luck, you'll get to hop on a shuttle and head into the woods to view this dazzling spectacle.

Towering Tree Houses

Minister's Tree House

Crossville Ⓝ 35.9853 Ⓦ 84.9944

According to Minister Horace Burgess, in 1993, God appeared to him in a vision and ordered him to build a tree house. A *huge* tree house. So Horace got to work.

More than 20 years later, the Minister's Tree House is a castle in the sky. It sprawls across seven trees in the woods of central Tennessee and is 97 feet (29.6 m) tall—as high as a nine-story building. It has at least 80 rooms, plus balconies, peaked roofs, and even a bell tower.

Horace believes that everyone should be allowed in his tree house. Recently, though, the Tennessee fire marshal closed it because it didn't comply with official safety rules. You may not be able to climb inside this colossal structure, but its design may inspire you when you think about building your own castle in the sky.

Korowai
Tree Houses

Trunyan
Cemetery

INDONESIA

LOCATION: made up of more than 13,000 islands in the Indian and Pacific Oceans

POPULATION: 263.7 million, the fourth largest on Earth

GEOGRAPHICAL FEATURE: The Sidoarjo Mud Volcano belches out about 65,398 cubic yards (50,000 m³) of mud each day.

OBSCURE FACT: It's home to both the world's largest lizard (the Komodo dragon) and largest flower (*Rafflesia arnoldii*, which smells like rotting meat).

Towering Tree Houses
Korowai Tree Houses
Kia, Papua Ⓢ 6.5933 Ⓔ 140.1636

Imagine waking up every morning in the trees. That's how the Korowai people of Papua start their days. These incredibly skilled architects build their homes out of natural materials like logs and palm fronds. Many houses can support up to a dozen people and sit as high as a three-story building. Some reach a whopping ten stories.

Why live in a tree house? It's not just for fun. Far above the steamy jungle, these hunter-gatherers are safe from mosquitoes and human intruders. The only way to enter some of their houses is by scaling a single dangling pole. As you climb, the pole wobbles, signaling to the people in the house that somebody's coming.

For a long time, nobody in the outside world knew about the Korowai people. That changed in the 1970s when Dutch missionaries encountered them. Since then, many Korowai have moved into nearby towns, and only a few thousand remain in the jungle.

Secrets of Skeletons

Trunyan Cemetery

Trunyan, Bali ⓢ 8.2444 ⓔ 115.4263

You've probably never visited a cemetery like the one in Trunyan. To get there, sail across a cool, clear lake below an active volcano on the beautiful island of Bali. When you step off the boat and enter the cemetery, you won't see any gravestones around you. Instead, you'll find skulls. *Tons* of skulls. They're stacked in huge piles on rocks along with other human bones.

    The villagers in Trunyan don't bury their family members in graves. Instead, they leave the bodies in bamboo huts or right out in the open in the shade of an enormous tree. To the villagers, the giant tree, a type of fig tree called a banyan, is sacred. The cemetery is full of bodies, so it should smell like decaying matter. But it doesn't, perhaps thanks to the banyan tree's pleasantly spicy leaves.

See more surprising skeletons at India's Roopkund Lake, 16,500 feet (5,029 m) above sea level. There are no roads, so hire a guide, plus a mule to carry supplies for the four-day trek!

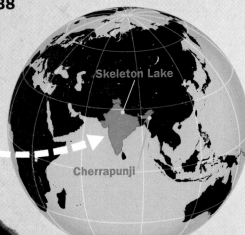

INDIA

LOCATION: southern Asia, sticking out into the Indian Ocean

POPULATION: 1.3 billion, the second largest on Earth (only to China)

NATIONAL ANIMAL: Bengal tiger

OBSCURE FACT: The Indian space agency was the first to put a spacecraft in orbit around Mars on the first try.

Secrets of Skeletons

Skeleton Lake

Roopkund, Uttarakhand Ⓝ 30.2620 Ⓔ 79.7320

In 1942, a park ranger made a gruesome discovery high up in the Himalayan Mountains. He stumbled upon a frozen lake surrounded by human bones. Two hundred people died here. What killed them? For decades, nobody had any idea.

See if *you* can solve the mystery of Roopkund Lake. Here are the facts: According to scientists, the victims were killed nearly 1,200 years ago. They all died from blows to the head that came from above. But nobody ever found any murder weapons. So what happened?

A 2004 expedition to the lake uncovered the surprising answer. The killer was likely a powerful hailstorm. Of course, hail is rarely deadly. In this case, the chunks of ice were as big as tennis balls. The victims were caught in the open, unable to reach shelter as the hail plummeted down. You can still find their remains today when you trek up to the lake. Just keep your eyes peeled for weird weather.

Beautiful Bridges

Root Bridges of Cherrapunji

Cherrapunji, Meghalaya Ⓝ 25.3000 Ⓔ 91.7000

When the Khasi people of northeast India need to cross a river, they don't build a bridge. They *grow* one. Their living bridges are made almost entirely of tree roots.

First, they lay out hollow trunks to help guide rubber-tree roots across the water. The roots start out thin and weak, but they slowly grow thicker. As the bridge takes shape, the Khasi pour mud and place stones into the gaps. Then they hang vines along the sides for handrails.

Growing a root bridge is difficult and can take decades. So why go to all this trouble? The Khasi live in one of the world's wettest places. During the monsoon season, the swollen streams are treacherous, and people can't wade through them to reach nearby villages. A typical wooden bridge would rot. A living root bridge, on the other hand, can last for centuries. It gets stronger over time and supports the weight of up to 50 people.

At a distance of 11,110 miles (17,880 km) away in Peru, there's a bridge made entirely of grass. You can't cross a root bridge to get there, but if you could, the walk might take you five months.

PERU

LOCATION: western South America on the Pacific Ocean

FOOD: Guinea pigs, native to Peru, are a traditional delicacy.

GEOGRAPHICAL FEATURE: Cerro Blanco, one of the world's highest sand dunes at 3,860 feet (1,177 m)

OBSCURE FACT: Tambopata National Reserve has more species of birds (595) than any similarly sized place on the planet. Look for parrots that mysteriously snack on clay.

Keshwa Chaca

Nazca Lines

Beautiful Bridges

Keshwa Chaca Rope Bridge

Huinchiri, Cusco Ⓢ 14.3831 Ⓦ 71.4933

You're standing at the edge of a steep gorge, staring down at the Apurímac River 60 feet (18.3 m) below. To cross, you'll have to put your trust in a bridge made entirely of . . . grass?! But don't worry. That bridge is strong enough to hold you, plus 55 of your closest friends.

The Keshwa Chaca is the last remaining Incan grass bridge. Masters of weaving fiber, the Inca sailed in ships made of reeds and wore cotton armor. Long before Europeans figured out how to build suspension bridges centuries ago, Incas were hanging hundreds of rope bridges across canyons.

Those bridges have vanished, but the Keshwa Chaca lives on. That's because local people rebuild it every year. They toss the old bridge in the river and work together to braid a new one. This act keeps them connected to their past, just as the bridge connects the two sides of the gorge.

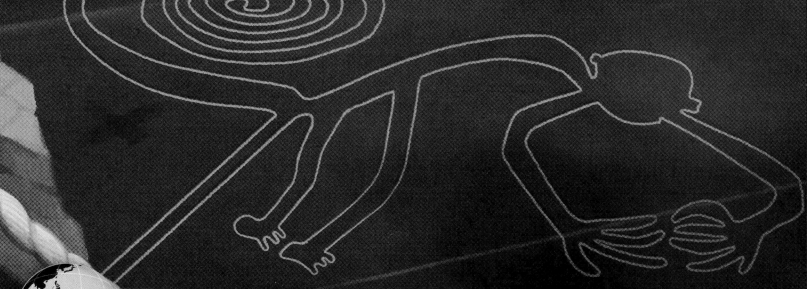

Ginormous Geoglyphs
Nazca Lines
Nazca, Ica ⓢ 14.6976 ⓦ 75.1265

Head west into the flat, dusty Nazca Desert and you'll find huge lines scratched into the dry earth. If you look closely, you'll notice that they seem to form shapes. To see them fully, though, you'll have to take to the sky.

Book a flight from a nearby town. From high above, you'll discover that these shapes are land designs called *geoglyphs*. Some are geometric shapes, and others are enormous animals: a monkey, a hummingbird, a whale, a spider, and more. The largest creature, a pelican, is as long as three football fields.

The Nazca people created this giant zoo by hand between 400 and 650 CE, long before the invention of the first airplane. Why make art you can't see? Perhaps the Nazca were trying to send messages to their gods high above.

Find another enormous geoglyph in South Australia's scorching outback, 8,685 miles (13,977 km) away across the South Pacific Ocean. Why not paddle there on a *caballito de totora*, a traditional Peruvian boat made of reeds?

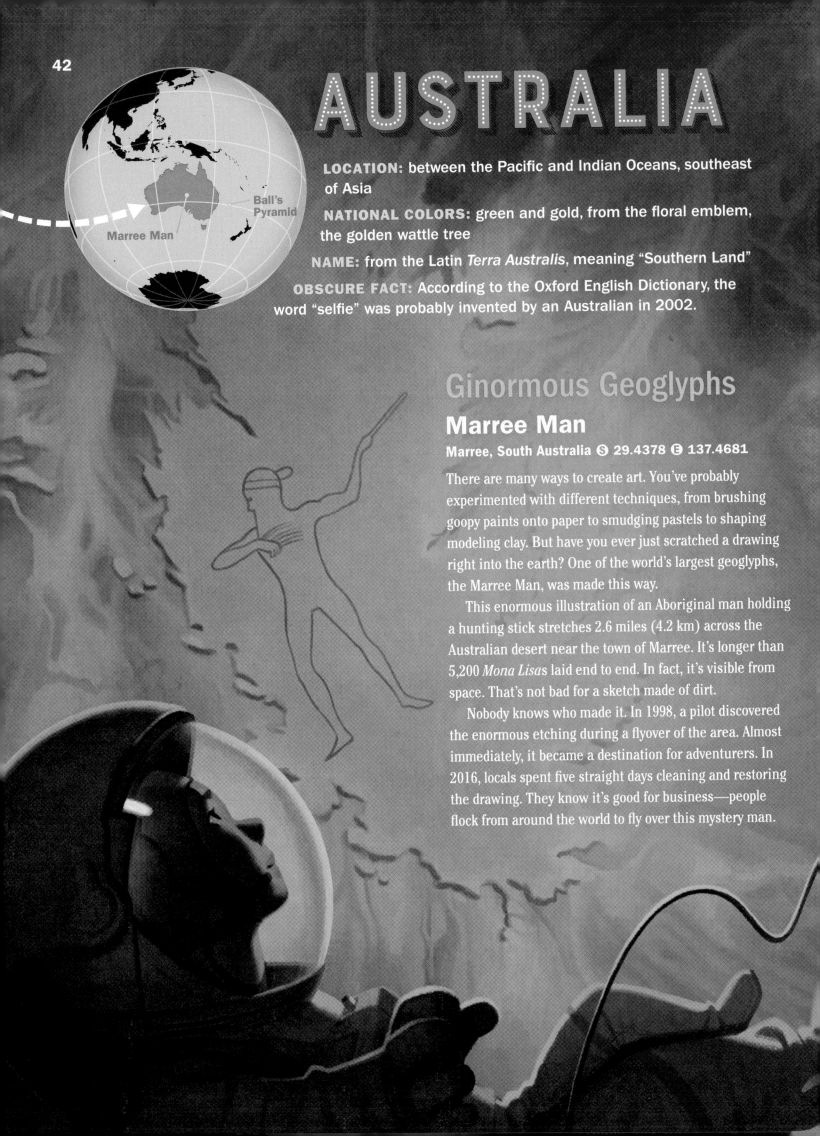

AUSTRALIA

LOCATION: between the Pacific and Indian Oceans, southeast of Asia

NATIONAL COLORS: green and gold, from the floral emblem, the golden wattle tree

NAME: from the Latin *Terra Australis*, meaning "Southern Land"

OBSCURE FACT: According to the Oxford English Dictionary, the word "selfie" was probably invented by an Australian in 2002.

Ginormous Geoglyphs

Marree Man

Marree, South Australia Ⓢ **29.4378** Ⓔ **137.4681**

There are many ways to create art. You've probably experimented with different techniques, from brushing goopy paints onto paper to smudging pastels to shaping modeling clay. But have you ever just scratched a drawing right into the earth? One of the world's largest geoglyphs, the Marree Man, was made this way.

This enormous illustration of an Aboriginal man holding a hunting stick stretches 2.6 miles (4.2 km) across the Australian desert near the town of Marree. It's longer than 5,200 *Mona Lisa*s laid end to end. In fact, it's visible from space. That's not bad for a sketch made of dirt.

Nobody knows who made it. In 1998, a pilot discovered the enormous etching during a flyover of the area. Almost immediately, it became a destination for adventurers. In 2016, locals spent five straight days cleaning and restoring the drawing. They know it's good for business—people flock from around the world to fly over this mystery man.

Animal Islands

Ball's Pyramid

Lord Howe Island Group ⓢ 31.7542 ⓔ 159.2571

Lord Howe Island, off the east coast of Australia, was once crawling with giant prehistoric-looking insects. Called Lord Howe Island phasmids—and nicknamed "tree lobsters"—these harmless creatures grew as long as a human hand. They were so common that people used them as fishing bait.

In 1918, disaster struck. A rat-infested British ship ran aground on Lord Howe Island. The rats spread across the landscape, eating everything in their path, insects included. Just two years later, the Lord Howe Island phasmid was extinct.

Or was it?

Southeast of Lord Howe Island, there's a steep, barren peak called Ball's Pyramid, the remnant of an ancient volcano. No people live here. In 2001, biologists investigating the island found a few surviving phasmids clinging to a single bush. They captured some of them to breed in zoos. With luck, perhaps tree lobsters will one day return to Lord Howe Island.

Fly into São Paolo, Brazil, to see another island with rare animals. It's about 20 miles (32 km) off the coast. Just don't

BRAZIL

LOCATION: eastern South America along the Atlantic Ocean

AREA: South America's largest nation at 3,287,956 square miles (8,515,767 km²) and fifth largest in the world

SPORTS: Brazil has the world's most successful World Cup soccer team, with five titles.

OBSCURE FACT: You can enjoy a performance at Teatro Amazonas, an opera house in the heart of the rain forest.

Old Petrolândia

Snake Island

Animal Islands

Snake Island

Ilha da Queimada Grande, São Paulo
Ⓢ 24.4879 Ⓦ 46.6742

Sail past this small island off the coast of São Paulo and you won't see anything unusual— just rocky shores and a blanket of trees. But the Brazilian government will only let you land here if you're accompanied by a doctor. There's a pretty good reason: This island is crawling with more venomous snakes per square foot than anywhere else on Earth.

They aren't just *any* snakes. Called golden lanceheads, they're found only on Snake Island. They sit in trees and ambush migratory birds, injecting flesh-dissolving venom into them. Perhaps 2,000 to 4,000 snakes inhabit the island, which spans 0.16 square miles (0.4 km²), just a little larger than Disneyland.

At one time, there were even *more* snakes. Sadly (for the snakes), they've suffered from habitat destruction and disease. Also, poachers capture lanceheads and sell them on the black market to collectors. On Snake Island, the greatest threat may be *us*.

Sunken Cities

Old Petrolândia

Petrolândia, Pernambuco ⓢ 9.0213 ⓦ 38.2651

In remote northeastern Brazil, an old church sits in the middle of a river. The floor is totally submerged, but the beautiful arched ceiling rises above the rushing water. Who built this sunken church, and why?

At one time, the church stood on dry land. It was constructed to serve the people of a town called Petrolândia in a valley near the São Francisco River. In the late 1970s and 1980s, the government built an enormous dam on the river to generate power. This project flooded the valley, and thousands of people had to leave their homes. Soon the water rose above every building—except the top of that church.

Petrolândia's villagers moved nearby and founded a new town of the same name on the shoreline of the flooded river. The only sign of Old Petrolândia is the church's remains, now a gathering place for fish instead of parishioners.

Explore a far older sunken city 5,306 miles (8,539 km) across the Atlantic in Africa. It's off the coast of Egypt's second largest city, Alexandria, named for the conqueror Alexander the Great.

EGYPT

LOCATION: northeast Africa and southwest Asia

CAPITAL: Cairo, Africa's second largest city (after Lagos, Nigeria)

GEOGRAPHICAL FEATURE: More than 90 percent of the land is desert. Most people live along the Nile River.

OBSCURE FACT: Ancient Egyptian men and women wore thick black and green eye makeup.

Heracleion

White Desert

Sunken Cities
The Lost City of Heracleion
Abu Qir Bay Ⓝ 31.3484 Ⓔ 30.1759

According to ancient texts, a bustling city called Heracleion flourished 2,300 years ago on Egypt's coast. Then it simply vanished. For centuries, archaeologists searched in vain for the ruins of this city.

In 2000, a team of archaeologists dove into the Mediterranean Sea near Alexandria. They came face-to-face with a huge stone statue. Soon they'd uncovered a temple, ships, gold coins, jewelry, and much more. At last, here were the ruins of Heracleion. The city had sunk beneath the waves.

How did such a thriving town wind up underwater? Heracleion was built on unstable soil, so the ground began sinking. At the same time, the sea level rose, flooding the streets. Tidal waves from earthquakes may have washed over the city, too.

Heracleion was doomed. But it wasn't lost forever. These days, archaeologists are working hard to haul its treasures back up to the surface for all to see and enjoy.

Colorful Geology
White Desert

Al Farafra, Western Desert ⊗ 27.0983 ⊕ 27.9858

Take a five-hour drive southwest from Cairo and you'll find a landscape like no other. In the White Desert, pale stone sculptures loom above the caramel-colored sand. You'll see mushrooms, trees, a camel, a chicken, and even an ice-cream cone.

Who created these statues? Nobody. These are *ventifacts*: rocks shaped by windblown sand. During the Cretaceous period, this area was a warm ocean. Tiny shelled creatures died and sank to the sea floor. The weight of sediment crushed their shells into chalk. Over time, as the continents moved and the climate changed, a desert was born. Strong winds swept up sand and scoured away that soft chalk.

Why do many of the formations look like mushrooms? Sand is heavy, so wind can't lift it very high, and it sandpapers the lowest rock first. This leaves large boulders teetering at the top of absurdly thin stems.

From the milk-white rock of the White Desert, head east to a place covered in chocolate-brown hills. You'll find it on tropical Bohol, the tenth largest island of the Philippines.

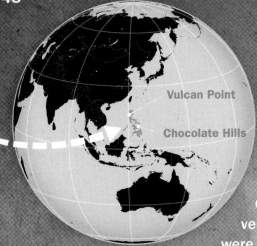

Vulcan Point

Chocolate Hills

PHILIPPINES

LOCATION: more than 7,000 islands in Southeast Asia

NAME: from a Spanish explorer, in honor of Spain's King Philip II

NATIONAL BIRD: Philippine eagle, a critically endangered bird that hunts monkeys

OBSCURE FACT: Jeepneys—crowded, beautifully decorated vehicles—serve as popular public transportation. The earliest ones were repurposed American military jeeps from World War II.

Colorful Geology
Chocolate Hills
Sierra Bullones Ⓝ 9.9167 Ⓔ 124.1667

The 214 steps to the lookout might leave you winded, but you'll forget your exhaustion the moment you reach the top and gaze across the Chocolate Hills. Hundreds of cone-shaped mounds poke up above the forest. They look like perfect dollops of pudding, or perhaps cocoa-dusted truffles. Mmm.

Sadly, you can't scoop them up with a spoon. They're made of limestone from the shells of ancient marine critters. As water flowed over and through them millions of years ago, it smoothed them into lumps. In fact, these hills only appear chocolaty during the dry season: That's when their blanket of grass goes from green to brown.

Their strange shape has inspired tons of legends. One of the most interesting—and disgusting—is about a giant water buffalo. When the beast destroyed crops, the angry locals gave it rotten food. Stricken with tummy troubles, it left mounds of poop all over the landscape.

Places Within Places
Vulcan Point

Volcano Lake, Luzon Ⓝ 14.0093 Ⓔ 120.9961

Have you ever played with a Russian nesting doll? It's a small doll inside a larger doll inside a larger doll . . . and so on. Vulcan Point is like a giant version of this toy. It's an island in the middle of a lake in the middle of an island in the middle of a lake in the middle of an island in the middle of the ocean. Try saying *that* five times fast!

The island of Vulcan Point is made of debris spewed out by a volcano called Taal. It sits in a lake at the center of the volcano. Taal is surrounded by a larger body of water, Taal Lake. That lake is on an island called Luzon in the Pacific Ocean.

When you hike through this rare geographic nesting doll, be forewarned: Taal Volcano is active and restless. Since the sixteenth century, it has erupted more than thirty times, sometimes with deadly results.

Sail northeast across the ocean on a *paraw*, a traditional Filipino boat, to find a geographic nesting doll in Japan with two volcanoes. Watch out for typhoons during the late spring, summer, and fall!

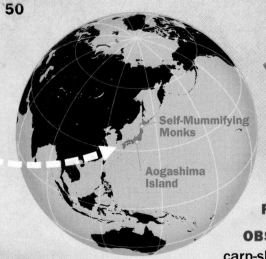

Self-Mummifying Monks

Aogashima Island

JAPAN

LOCATION: 6,852 islands in the Pacific Ocean off the east coast of Asia

CAPITAL: The greater Tokyo metropolitan area is the world's largest city, with about 38 million people.

FOOD: It's considered polite to loudly slurp your noodles.

OBSCURE FACT: On May 5, people celebrate Children's Day by flying carp-shaped banners—one fish for each kid in a family.

Places Within Places

Aogashima Island

Aogashima, Izu Islands Ⓝ 32.4583 Ⓔ 139.7688

You've already visited some astonishing volcanoes. But you've never seen anything quite like Aogashima. The whole island is one huge volcano—and there's a smaller volcano inside it.

The smaller volcano is a cinder cone. Here, lava spewed up from a central vent, solidified in the air, shattered into pieces, and fell in this shape. The larger crater is a caldera, and it formed when a volcano released its magma and collapsed inward. And that's just part of the story.

The island of Aogashima is built from the remains of at least *four* previous volcanoes.

As you can imagine, life on Aogashima has its drawbacks. In 1785, a violent eruption wiped out almost half the island's population. Fortunately, the volcano has been quiet since then. Its heat provides free power. It also warms water, creating natural saunas. When you visit one, bring a raw egg. You can boil it in a pan on top of a steam vent and enjoy a snack while you soak.

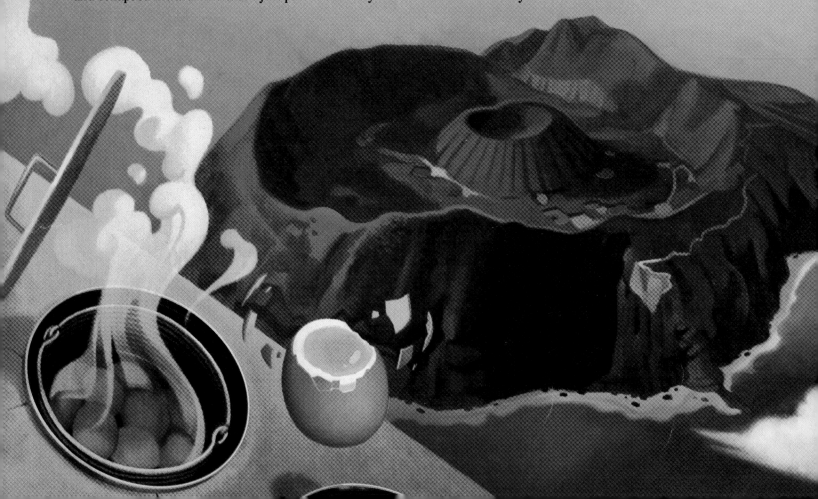

Meet the Mummies
Self-Mummifying Monks
Mount Yudono, Yamagata Ⓝ 38.5320 Ⓔ 139.9851

The most famous mummies are those from ancient Egypt. For the Egyptians, turning bodies into carefully preserved mummies required a team of artisans and embalmers. But between the eleventh and nineteenth centuries, a group of Japanese monks took a more "do-it-yourself" approach. They mummified *themselves*.

As you can probably guess, turning yourself into a mummy isn't fun. Here's how you do it. First, spend a thousand days exercising heavily and eating nuts and seeds. Then, switch to a diet of salt water and a toxic tea meant to make you pee a lot so you'll dry out. Finally, lock yourself in a pitch-black underground tomb.

Even after all this preparation, some monks would just rot away. There are 16 well-preserved monks left in Japan. You'll find one of the oldest at Dainichibo temple in Yamagata. He sits in a serene cross-legged position, just as he did when he died in 1783.

Some mummies don't just sit—they dance. See them 5,306 miles (8,539 km) away in France. If you could cross that distance in Japan's famous high-speed trains, you'd arrive in just 30.5 hours.

FRANCE

LOCATION: western Europe on both the Mediterranean Sea and the Atlantic Ocean

NATIONAL MOTTO: *Liberté, égalité, fraternité*—liberty, equality, and fraternity

ECONOMY: France is the world's most popular tourist destination.

OBSCURE FACT: The tomb of science fiction author Jules Verne features a sculpture of the writer rising from his grave.

Musée Fragonard

Eiffel Tower Apartment

Meet the Mummies

Musée Fragonard

Paris Ⓝ 48.8127 Ⓔ 2.4223

Usually, mummified bodies look peaceful, like they've found eternal rest. The ones at the Musée Fragonard in a suburb of Paris are different. Some are frozen in mid-dance. One rides a galloping horse (also mummified). But these aren't the only preserved bodies in this museum. You'll also come face-to-face with mutant animals, including a two-headed cow and a ten-legged sheep.

These creepy corpses are the creations of Professor Honoré Fragonard. In 1766, while working at a veterinary school, Fragonard perfected a technique for preserving bodies. He hoped to use his mummies to teach anatomy.

Not everyone was thrilled, though. The head of the school accused Fragonard of being insane and fired him. Lucky for Fragonard, wealthy people were big fans of his art. They paid him to preserve creatures that they could display in their mansions. Would you add a mummy to your living room?

Hidden in Plain Sight

Eiffel Tower Apartment

Paris Ⓝ 48.8583 Ⓔ 2.2945

Millions of people visit the Eiffel Tower every year. But few of them know about the secret apartment.

The Eiffel Tower's creator, Gustave Eiffel, built himself a private space on the third level, 1,000 feet (305 m) up. It had cozy furniture and even a piano. Here, Eiffel performed scientific experiments and entertained illustrious guests, including Thomas Edison and nobles from around the world. As soon as the people of Paris found out about this hideaway, they were severely jealous. At the time, the Eiffel Tower was the highest structure in the world, with spectacular views of the city below. Wealthy people offered to pay a fortune to spend just one night in the apartment.

Eiffel refused. He loved having his own personal sky-high space. If you go up the tower today, you'll be allowed to peek into the apartment. There you'll find lifelike wax figures of Eiffel, his daughter, and Thomas Edison.

To discover something else hidden in plain sight, travel 6,035 miles (9,712 km) to a massive temple in Cambodia. These two countires have a complex history: Cambodia gained independence from France in 1953 after 90 years of colonial rule.

CAMBODIA

LOCATION: southeast Asia on the Indochinese Peninsula

NATIONAL BIRD: giant ibis, a critically endangered species

FLAG: portrays the temple complex of Angkor Wat, the largest religious monument in the world

OBSCURE FACT: In Cambodia, the human head is considered sacred—never touch or pat somebody on the head!

Dinosaur of Ta Prohm

Bamboo Trains

Hidden in Plain Sight
Dinosaur of Ta Prohm
Angkor, Siem Reap Ⓝ 13.4350 Ⓔ 103.8892

Full of tall towers and exquisite carvings, the 900-year-old stone ruins at Angkor are wildly popular with tourists. But most visitors miss one of Angkor's weirder mysteries. In a quiet part of a ruined temple lurks . . . a dinosaur.

To find it, enter the Ta Prohm temple and turn left. On one wall, you'll see a stone carving of an animal with plates down its back. It looks a lot like a stegosaurus. Of course, dinosaurs went extinct 66 million years ago. So what's a dino carving doing on a 900-year-old ruin?

To some people, it's proof that ancient reptiles still roam the lush Cambodian jungle. Others think it's a modern hoax. Many believe that the "plates" are just plants and the animal is a present-day creature like a rhino. They're almost certainly right. Still, if you turn a corner at Angkor and encounter a living, breathing dinosaur, don't say you weren't warned.

DIY Transportation

Bamboo Trains

Battambang, Battambang Ⓝ 13.0688' Ⓔ 103.2022'

When years of war damaged Cambodia's rail system, locals took matters into their own hands. They *built their own trains*. You can hitch a ride on one of these homemade vehicles, or "norries," on the one remaining track. Just don't expect a smooth ride. In fact, bring a cushion to protect your butt.

Made of spare parts, a norry is basically a bamboo plank with a small motor from a tractor or motorcycle. It has four wheels that fit onto the old overgrown rail tracks. Hop on board and you may find yourself sitting next to chickens and dogs that are tagging along for the ride. Once the motor begins to whir, you're off on a twisty, tooth-rattling trip.

Sometimes two norries meet on the track. Then you'll witness these homemade trains' true power. The passengers hop off, take the norry apart, and rebuild it on the other side.

Discover more daredevil do-it-yourself transportation in Guayabetal, Colombia. It's near the antipode, which is a term for a place that's on the opposite side of the world from another place.

COLOMBIA

LOCATION: northwestern South America

FOOD: Colombians are big coffee consumers, and even kids drink coffee here.

COAT OF ARMS: features the national bird, a huge vulture called the Andean condor

OBSCURE FACT: At Volcán de Lodo El Totumo, you can relax in a naturally heated mud bath inside a volcano.

DIY Transportation

Homemade Zip Lines

Guayabetal, Cundinamarca Ⓝ 4.2209 Ⓦ 73.8166

For generations, kids in parts of the Andes Mountains used a surprising method to get to school. They used zip lines to cross gorges that were too wide for bridges. They'd zoom across the canyons at heart-pounding speeds of up to 60 miles an hour (97 kph). It was dangerous, but the alternative wasn't great, either: Kids would have to spend hours hiking through the steep forest to school.

Not all Colombians loved those zip lines, though. In the late 1990s, a popular TV news show shared the story of a six-year-old boy who rode one to school in the town of Guayabetal. Viewers were outraged that children were taking such dangerous trips. In response, the government yanked out all but four of the lines—and built a school on the boy's side of the gorge. Despite the uproar, a few brave kids still ride zip lines every morning.

Rainbow Waterways

Caño Cristales

La Macarena, Meta (N) 2.1830 (W) 73.7858

This may be the most beautiful river in the world. Peer into Caño Cristales—Spanish for "Crystal Channel"—and you'll see a dazzling rainbow of reds, purples, yellows, and greens mixing in round potholes and tumbling in waterfalls.

Most of this color comes from a humble river weed called *Macarenia clavigera*. It grows nowhere else on the planet. For a short period, from September to November, it blushes with pinks and reds. Combined with the yellow river sands, emerald trees, and blue waters, it creates a rich palette of colors that would make any artist jealous.

The plant is delicate, though. To protect it, the government allows just 200 people to visit per day. Watch where you swim—and don't step in the weeds.

Visit Yellowstone National Park for another splash of color. If you could string a huge Colombian zip line from here

WYOMING

LOCATION: western United States, partly in the Rocky Mountains

STATE DINOSAUR: triceratops

STATE SPORT: rodeo

OBSCURE FACT: Isa Lake is the world's only natural lake that drains into both the Atlantic and Pacific Oceans.

Rainbow Waterways

Grand Prismatic Spring

Yellowstone National Park Ⓝ 44.5251 Ⓦ 110.8382

Grand Prismatic Spring in Yellowstone National Park looks like a rainbow that crashed to Earth and pooled into a smoldering crater. If you like colors, you'll fall head over heels for it. Just *don't fall in*.

Heated by magma below the Earth's surface, the spring's mineral-rich waters bubble up through a crack in the ground. If you stepped into the pool, you'd get cooked. In fact, more people die from falling into Yellowstone's hot springs than are killed by the park's famous grizzly bears!

But certain bacteria and microbes, called thermophiles, adore these tough conditions. They cake the walls of the pool and give it rainbow hues. Visit the spring in different seasons and you'll notice the colors changing as various types of bacteria thrive and fade.

Self-Built Structures

Smith Mansion

Cody Ⓝ **44.4610** Ⓦ **109.4943**

If you built your own house from scraps of wood, without any blueprints or plans, it might look something like the Smith Mansion. Standing five stories tall, the structure is covered with balconies and packed with twisty staircases and unfinished rooms. There's a giant indoor swing, a table made of an enormous tree stump, and even a basketball court.

Engineer Francis Lee Smith built the whole thing by himself. He couldn't have picked a more beautiful place for a home. East of Yellowstone National Park in the Wapiti Valley, it's surrounded by sparsely populated, picturesque hills straight out of a Western movie.

Unfortunately, Smith didn't wear safety equipment while he worked on his house. In 1992 he fell from a balcony and died. Now his home sits empty. But it's much more than a building: It's a true work of art, amazing locals and visitors alike.

Francis Smith would have liked Don Justo, a Spaniard who built his own church. See Don Justo's creation by visiting Spain's capital, Madrid, and hopping on the *interurbano* bus #341 to the town of Mejorada del Campo.

SPAIN

LOCATION: southwest Europe on both the Atlantic Ocean and the Mediterranean Sea

NATIONAL ANTHEM: "Marcha Real," which has no words

GEOGRAPHICAL FEATURE: Ses Fonts Ufanes, a rushing stream that bubbles up from the ground after heavy rain, then vanishes

OBSCURE FACT: On New Year's Eve, for good luck, people try to eat twelve grapes as a clock tower chimes twelve times.

Self-Built Structures

Don Justo's Cathedral

Mejorada del Campo, Madrid Ⓝ 40.3946 Ⓦ 3.4885

At first glance, this seems like an ordinary church. But look closely. The columns are made of plastic buckets filled with concrete and topped with car tires. The walls are lined with newspaper. This is a cathedral of trash.

Incredibly, it's largely the work of just one man. Don Justo Gallego Martínez was once a deeply dedicated monk. In the early 1960s, he came down with a nasty disease called tuberculosis and had to leave his monastery so he wouldn't sicken anyone else.

Still faithful and dedicated—and now very bored—Don Justo decided to build a recycled cathedral all by himself in the small town of Mejorada del Campo near Madrid. He's been working on it ever since. He's now in his nineties, and probably won't live to see it completed. But he'd like to be buried in the basement. In fact, he's already dug his own grave there.

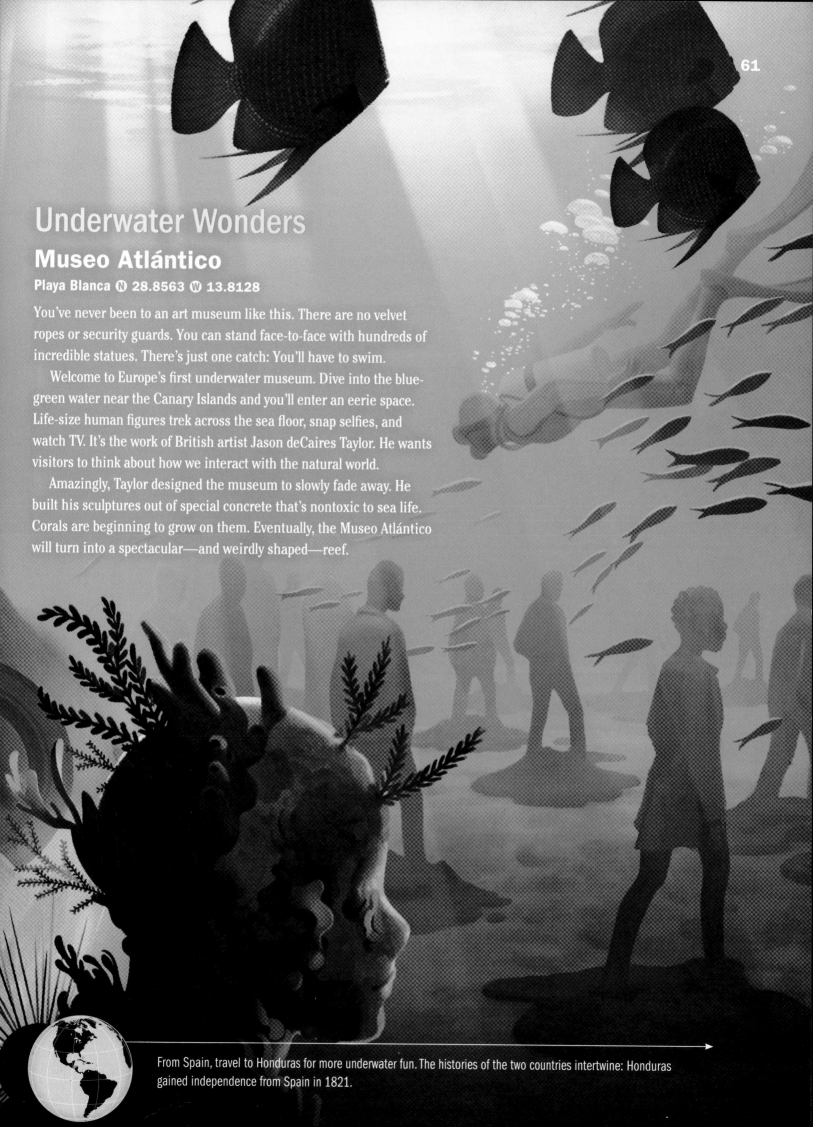

Underwater Wonders
Museo Atlántico
Playa Blanca Ⓝ 28.8563 Ⓦ 13.8128

You've never been to an art museum like this. There are no velvet ropes or security guards. You can stand face-to-face with hundreds of incredible statues. There's just one catch: You'll have to swim.

Welcome to Europe's first underwater museum. Dive into the blue-green water near the Canary Islands and you'll enter an eerie space. Life-size human figures trek across the sea floor, snap selfies, and watch TV. It's the work of British artist Jason deCaires Taylor. He wants visitors to think about how we interact with the natural world.

Amazingly, Taylor designed the museum to slowly fade away. He built his sculptures out of special concrete that's nontoxic to sea life. Corals are beginning to grow on them. Eventually, the Museo Atlántico will turn into a spectacular—and weirdly shaped—reef.

From Spain, travel to Honduras for more underwater fun. The histories of the two countries intertwine: Honduras gained independence from Spain in 1821.

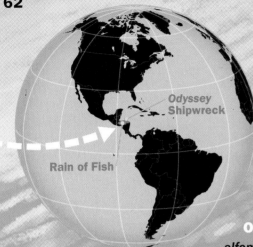

HONDURAS

LOCATION: Central America, touching both the Pacific Ocean and the Caribbean Sea

NATIONAL BIRD: scarlet macaw, a rainbow-colored parrot

NAME: from the Spanish word for "depths," because of the Bay of Trujillo's deep waters

OBSCURE FACT: At Comayagua, giant sawdust illustrations called *alfombras*, or carpets, are made in the streets and then trampled.

Underwater Wonders

The *Odyssey* Shipwreck

Roatán, Bay Islands Ⓝ 16.3455 Ⓦ 86.5542

In November 2002, a huge freighter ship—longer than seven buses parked end to end—was towed out to sea next to the island of Roatán. Workers deliberately opened hatches in the sides and stepped back as water filled the ship. It slowly sank 110 feet (34 m), coming to rest on the sandy seafloor.

Why sink a boat on purpose? You'll figure out the answer as soon as you pull on scuba gear and dive down. With towering walls and abundant sea life, the *Odyssey* is a diver's paradise.

This ship was once a successful freight-hauler—until a fire damaged it beyond repair. Its owners partnered with a nearby resort to sink the *Odyssey* so scuba enthusiasts could explore it. But diving into a wreck is notoriously dangerous. To make things safer, they added hunks of metal for strength and cut holes for exploration. Now it's a haven for sharks, barracuda, and happy divers.

Weird Weather

Rain of Fish

Yoro, Yoro Ⓝ 15.1333 Ⓦ 87.1423

According to legend, when it rains in the small town of Yoro, things get weird. Hundreds of silver fish tumble from the sky, bounce off your umbrella, and lie flopping on the sidewalk.

Does that rain of fish sound a little . . . fishy to you? You're not alone. In the 1970s, a group of National Geographic Society researchers visited Yoro to find out whether the legend was true. They saw fish all over the ground, but they never observed them falling from the sky.

Some people think that the fish live in dark streams below the streets. When heavy rainfall fills their rivers, they swim to the surface and wind up gasping on the sidewalk. No matter where the fish come from, the townspeople of Yoro take full advantage of this excuse for a party. They throw a festival every year in honor of the fish fall.

Go south to Venezuela to see a more "shocking" storm. To get there from here, take a boat or plane, but not a car: There are no roads through the dangerous Darién Gap between Panama and Colombia.

Coromoto
Ice Cream
Shop

Everlasting
Lightning
Storm

VENEZUELA

LOCATION: northern South America along the Atlantic Ocean

GEOGRAPHICAL FEATURE: Angel Falls, the planet's highest waterfall, is 3,212 feet (979 m) tall.

FOOD: The world's largest rodent, the capybara, is eaten here.

OBSCURE FACT: El Monumento a la Paz in the capital, Caracas, is a peace monument made of stones and recycled material.

Weird Weather

Everlasting Lightning Storm

Congo Mirador, Zulia Ⓝ 9.5632 Ⓦ 71.3824

Where the Catatumbo River meets Lake Maracaibo, you'll find some of the world's most shocking weather. Storm clouds bubble up and lightning begins to strike. And strike again. And strike some more. Hundreds of bolts flash every hour for up to *10 straight hours.*

In a strange way, this storm has kept the locals safe. In 1595, the English pirate Sir Francis Drake tried to invade the city of Maracaibo under cover of night, but lightning lit up his troops and spoiled the surprise. And in 1823, lightning exposed the position of Spanish ships during the Venezuelan War of Independence.

To witness this astonishing show, you'll sail to a lakeside village where the houses sit on stilts. Just pull up a chair and wait for the sun to sink. You'll need a little luck, though. The storm isn't *really* eternal, but it does appear about 260 nights a year.

Sweet Treats

Coromoto Ice Cream Shop

Mérida Ⓝ 8.5587 Ⓦ 71.2026

Ice cream for dinner? At the Heladería Coromoto, you can live the dream . . . or the nightmare. Savor a frosty spaghetti-flavored scoop. Try hot dog, sardine, onion, salmon, or garlic. Or enjoy a traditional Venezuelan meal of rice, beans, shredded beef, and plantain—all in the form of a frozen treat.

This ice cream shop offers more flavors than any other in the world. About 60 of the 900 varieties are on sale at any given time. If you're feeling less adventurous, you can try tropical, fruity tastes such as mango, coconut, and avocado. And of course, the classics: chocolate and vanilla. But where's the fun in that? The owner, Manuel da Silva Oliveira, wants to push the boundaries of taste— something that is hard to do these days as Venezuela faces scary food shortages. The shop sometimes closes due to lack of supplies, so if you're lucky enough to find it open, grab a cone.

HELADERIA COROMOTO
MERIDA

CO MOTO

What goes well with ice cream? Cookies! Taste some of the best in Toruń, Poland. You'll fly into an airport named after Ignacy Jan Paderewski, a prime minister—and famous musician.

POLAND

LOCATION: eastern Europe on the Baltic Sea

CULTURE: To celebrate the end of winter, kids make dolls of the winter goddess Marzanna, set them on fire, and toss them in a river.

FOOD: St. Martin's Croissant, a legally protected recipe

OBSCURE FACT: In the 1400s and 1500s, a popular red fabric dye was extracted from a local bug called the Polish cochineal.

Sweet Treats

Museum of Toruń Gingerbread

Toruń Ⓝ 53.0087 Ⓔ 18.6045

When you bite into a gingerbread cookie, you taste a treat that kids have enjoyed for thousands of years. The earliest known gingerbread recipes come from ancient Greece. During medieval times, people nibbled these spicy cookies at festivals and fairs. Queen Elizabeth I of England even employed her own official gingerbread maker in the 1500s.

The city of Toruń in northern Poland became famous for its traditional gingerbread. Huge cookie factories sprang up there during the 1800s. A man named Gustav Traugott Weese owned the largest. Today, Weese's house has become one sweet museum. Here you can discover the history of gingerbread and learn how it's made. You'll meet a peculiar cast of costumed characters, including bakers dressed in traditional garb. The best part? Using traditional methods, you'll bake your own delicious creations to take home and enjoy.

Salty Sensations

Wieliczka Salt Mine

Wieliczka, Lesser Poland
N 48.9830 E 20.0557

You're standing in an elegant chapel. Crystal chandeliers hang overhead, filling the room with a warm glow. Statues and columns line the walls. Incredibly, every part of it, from the smallest crystal to the largest column, is made of salt.

This chapel sits in a salt mine in southern Poland. Workers dug rock salt here for centuries. In their free time, they carved the dank caverns into spectacular art. Tourists started dropping by to admire their creative works. Nowadays, the halls are full of visitors. You can eat at a restaurant, visit a lake, and sleep over at a resort.

But you won't ever forget you're in a mine. There aren't any windows here. When your visit is done, you'll squeeze into a tiny miner's cage—a little like a rickety elevator—and slowly rise to the surface.

This isn't the only place where you can sleep surrounded by salt. To visit another, travel for 7,183 miles (11,560 km), crossing the equator and entering the Andes Mountains, the longest continental mountain range in the world.

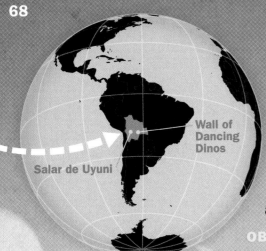

Salar de Uyuni

Wall of Dancing Dinos

BOLIVIA

LOCATION: central-west South America, landlocked by five countries

GEOGRAPHICAL FEATURE: Lake Titicaca, the highest navigable lake (shared with Peru)

NUMBER OF OFFICIAL LANGUAGES: 37, including Spanish and dozens of indigenous languages

OBSCURE FACT: On March 23, Bolivians recognize Day of the Sea, the anniversary of Bolivia losing its coastline in a nineteenth-century war with neighboring Chile.

Salty Sensations

Salar de Uyuni

Uyuni, Potosí ⓢ 20.2803 ⓦ 66.9825

Are you a fan of salt? When you sit down for dinner, do you sprinkle way too much of it on your food? If so, you need to visit Salar de Uyuni.

Thousands of years ago, a huge lake dried up here, leaving behind a white plain of glittering salt that covers thousands of square miles. During the rainy part of the year, the plain becomes a shallow lake. You can hop in a truck or a boat and splash your way to the middle. There you'll find a hotel that's almost entirely made of—okay, you guessed it—more salt.

The walls of the Hotel Luna Salada are built of salt bricks stuck together with salt mortar. The floor is salt. The chairs, tables, and beds are salt. It's pretty special, but you may find yourself yearning for other flavors. Pass the pepper, please.

Dinosaur Party

Wall of Dancing Dinos

Sucre Ⓢ 19.0028 Ⓦ 65.2372

The dinosaur dance floor in southern Bolivia is ancient evidence of a massive party. If you traveled back in time about 68 million years, you'd see more than eight types of dinos, from plant eaters to ferocious carnivores, all cavorting across a shallow lake.

Those partiers left behind thousands of footprints in wild patterns all over the lake bed. You see, over time, the mud turned into stone. Then something peculiar happened. The Earth's surface is broken up into enormous tectonic plates, and they move around, pulling apart and smashing into each other. This motion pushed the footprint-covered rock high into the air. Now the dance floor is a huge slanting wall. It's the largest known site of dino tracks, and today, you can walk right up to it. If you look closely, you'll notice one set of tracks that's more than 1,100 feet (335 m) long. Those footprints belong to a carnivorous baby dinosaur who must have *really* liked the party.

Keep the party going with a visit to a Scottish dino disco. If you rode there on a *T. rex*, it'd take you about 22 days—depending on how fast your tyrannosaur could swim across the ocean. (Buy some big floaties.)

Isle of Skye · Burning of the Clavie

SCOTLAND

LOCATION: western Europe on the northern part of the island of Great Britain

NATIONAL ANIMAL: unicorn

GEOGRAPHICAL FEATURE: Ben Nevis, the UK's highest peak at 4,409 feet (1,344 m)

OBSCURE FACT: The heart of Robert the Bruce, a national hero, warrior, and king, is buried in an abbey in Melrose.

Dinosaur Party

Dino Shindig on the Isle of Skye

Staffin, Skye Ⓝ 57.6824 Ⓦ 6.3396

When you think of Scotland, you may think of kilts, Loch Ness, and old castles shrouded in fog. From now on, you should also think of stomping Jurassic dinosaurs.

170 million years ago on the Isle of Skye, you'd find a very different Scotland. Standing along a seaside lagoon under the hot subtropical sun, you'd hear the thunderous footsteps of massive dinosaurs romping back and forth.

We know about these dinos because some lucky scientists happened to be in the right place at the right time to make an exceptionally rare paleontological discovery. As they walked by the sea when the tide was low, the receding water exposed rock pitted with potholes in peculiar zigzagging, crisscrossing patterns. These tracks belonged to sauropod dinosaurs—long-necked animals like *Brachiosaurus* that once frolicked by the seaside.

Fire Festivals

The Burning of the Clavie

Burghead, Moray Ⓝ 57.7002 Ⓦ 3.4892

Visit the small seaside town of Burghead on January 11 and you'll witness a strange and unique fiery festival. The villagers set a "clavie," or barrel, alight and parade it through the town. Then they dump it on an altar and snatch hot coals to take home as souvenirs.

Scottish people have a long history of warming up the winter with fire festivals. The tradition dates back to a time before Catholicism, when most people in what is now the United Kingdom held pagan beliefs. The Catholic Church wasn't a big fan of these ancient faiths. During the 1700s, it labeled the festival sinful and superstitious. It even changed the calendar so that New Year's Day no longer fell on January 11, a pagan holiday.

But the people of Burghead refused to give up their traditions. They still burn a big tar-filled barrel. Afterward, they use the coals to light their first cozy fires of the New Year.

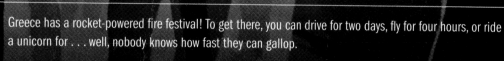

Greece has a rocket-powered fire festival! To get there, you can drive for two days, fly for four hours, or ride a unicorn for . . . well, nobody knows how fast they can gallop.

GREECE

LOCATION: southeast Europe on the Mediterranean Sea

NATIONAL ANTHEM: "Hymn to Liberty" contains 158 verses, the most text of any anthem.

HISTORY: Greek is one of the world's oldest written languages.

OBSCURE FACT: The island of Samos has caves where the ancient mathematician Pythagoras lived and taught.

Antikythera
Mechanism

Chios
Rocket War

Fire Festivals

Chios Rocket War

Vrontados, Chios Ⓝ 38.3710 Ⓔ 26.1363

There are all sorts of ways to celebrate Easter. You can paint eggs. You can eat chocolate (so long as you're not allergic). Or you can visit the Greek island of Chios and watch a pair of rival churches blast the living daylights out of each other with tens of thousands of dangerous homemade rockets.

Nobody knows when or why these two churches started their Easter war. Some say they used to fire cannons at each other instead, but the government outlawed the practice and took the cannons away.

Neither side ever "wins"—in fact, both sides declare themselves the winner and agree to fight again next year. But many villagers aren't thrilled about this tradition. The rockets blast houses, set fires, and fill the air with a choking smoke. Also, the people who launch them sometimes lose fingers—and even their lives.

Clockwork Computing

Antikythera Mechanism

Athens Ⓝ 37.9899 Ⓔ 23.7310

In 1900, divers were hunting for sponges off the Greek island of Antikythera when they came across a shipwreck. Nestled among the pieces of wreckage was something totally unexpected: a 2,000-year-old computer.

You might have a fancy computer—a cell phone—sitting right in your pocket. But the Antikythera mechanism, now held in the National Archaeological Museum of Athens, is something special. It's the earliest known computer by far. Nothing like it appears in the archaeological record for the next thousand years.

This intricate bronze machine calculates the positions of the planets and other astronomical bodies, and even the dates for the next Olympic games. To use it, you would enter a date by turning a wheel or a crank. Gears would turn, and dials revealed your answers. Like a cell phone, it's supposed to be portable, even though it's a huge hunk of bronze. Evidence suggests that people would carry it around in a wooden box and pop it out whenever they needed to do some computing.

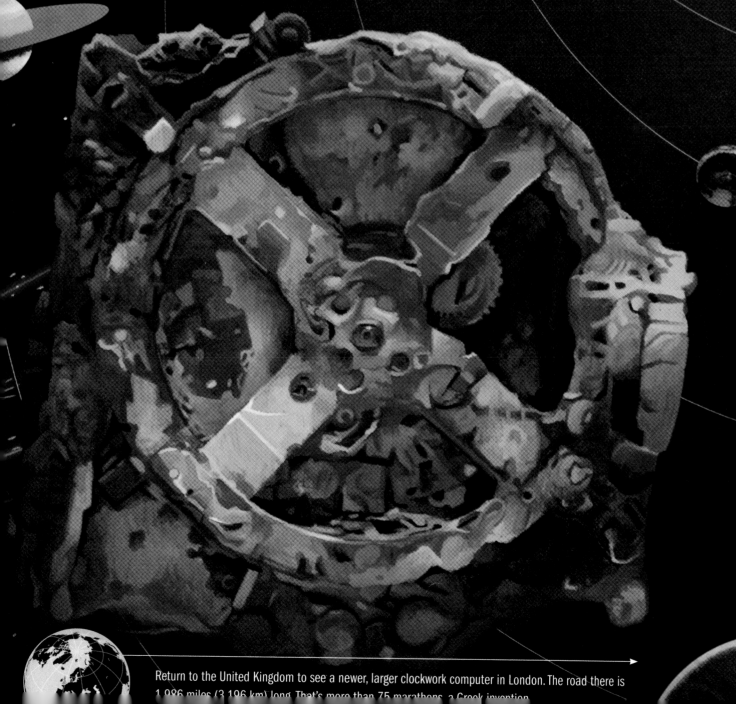

Return to the United Kingdom to see a newer, larger clockwork computer in London. The road there is 1,986 miles (3,196 km) long. That's more than 75 marathons, a Greek invention.

ENGLAND

LOCATION: northwest Europe on an island in the Atlantic Ocean

CULTURAL FEATURE: mysterious 4,600-year-old Avebury stones, the world's largest stone circle

NATIONAL FLOWER: rose

OBSCURE FACT: Until about 8,000 years ago, the sea levels were lower and you could walk from England to France.

Clockwork Computing

Difference Engine #2

London Ⓝ 51.4982 Ⓦ 0.1740

In 1822, a mathematician named Charles Babbage was feeling frustrated. He usually did his work with the help of printed, human-calculated math tables. But these charts were often full of mistakes. Rather than working out his frustration by taking a calming walk along the River Thames, Babbage sat down and designed a mechanical calculator for doing fast approximations.

These designs made Babbage famous. But he never lived to see them turned into working machines. They were just too complicated, and the technology and tools of the time simply weren't good enough.

Finally, in 1991, London's Science Museum built his most famous machine, the Difference Engine #2. It required 20 pages of complex blueprints and 25,000 finicky parts, from gears to rods to levers. The finished brass computer weighs as much as an elephant. It's a remarkable feat of ingenuity—but it's not exactly something you'd bring in your backpack to math class.

Micronations

Principality of Sealand

North Sea ⓝ 51.5342 ⓔ 1.2850

Have you ever wanted your own country? What would you name it? Hopefully you'd be a little more creative than Prince Roy Bates of Sealand. In 1967, Bates sailed to an abandoned World War II–era British sea fort and claimed it as a new nation. He called it Sealand because, well, it sits in the middle of the sea.

Sealand may be tiny, but it has its own currency, flag, and soccer team. Unfortunately, things haven't always gone smoothly here. In 1978, a German citizen landed at Sealand and tried to take it over. The Bates family recaptured it by helicopter. For a time, you could buy Sealand passports, but too many counterfeit ones kept showing up. Oh, and in 2006 the fort caught fire.

Sure, it has its problems. But Sealand also offers an easy route to becoming a nobleperson. Just pay a small fee— at only $40, lordships are a steal.

Sealand is just one of many tiny unofficial nations around the world. You won't need a passport to go see another nearby— just drive for 16 hours (and take two ferry rides) into Sweden.

SWEDEN

LOCATION: northern Europe on the Baltic Sea

POPULATION: 10 million, just half of the size of New York State's

CAPITAL: Stockholm, where the year's shortest night lasts less than five and a half hours

OBSCURE FACT: Fulufjället Mountain features Old Tjikko, a scraggly 9,550-year-old tree.

Micronations

Ladonia

Ladonia (N) 56.2863 (E) 12.5409

This nation has two national anthems, and one of them is the "bloop" of a stone thrown into water. The official language has only two words: *waaaall* and *ÿp*. Every clock runs three minutes behind those in neighboring Sweden. Welcome to the strange state of Ladonia.

This tiny nation was born from a battle over art. In 1980, sculptor Lars Vilks started creating an enormous driftwood structure on the rocky beach of a nature preserve. He named it *Nimis*, Latin for "too much." The government wasn't a fan of *Nimis*, though, because Vilks had built this huge sculpture without permission. Swedish officials ordered that it be destroyed.

Instead, Vilks protected it by declaring the land around it a new country. He named his artwork Ladonia and developed a currency, a flag, and more. Anyone in the world—yes, you too—can become a citizen of this tiny seaside state. Just be aware that no other country recognizes it as a real nation!

Small Worlds
Little Istanbul
Sala, Västmanland Ⓝ 59.9217 Ⓔ 16.5578

From that tiny nation, travel northeast and you'll find a tiny city. Nestled in a Swedish backyard are miniature versions of Istanbul's most famous buildings.

   Their creator, Jan-Erik Swennberg, has Asperger's syndrome. People with Asperger's often become intensely fascinated with a particular subject. In Swennberg's case, it's Turkish architecture. In 1979, he went on a holiday in Istanbul and fell head over heels for the intricate palaces, tall towers, and colorful mosques.

   When Swennberg got home, he couldn't stop thinking about those buildings. So he decided to make his own backyard versions. His first sculpture was the Sultan Ahmed Mosque, known as the Blue Mosque because of its sky-blue tiles. Now his backyard is a tiny city of colorful, incredibly detailed structures, all made of recycled material.

To see thousands of buildings, cars, and bicycles on an even smaller scale—about three times smaller than Little Istanbul, in fact—head to southern Germany on your normal-sized bicycle. You'll arrive after just 52 hours of pedaling.

Wunderland
Kalkar

Miniatur
Wunderland

GERMANY

LOCATION: west-central Europe, north of Austria and Switzerland and south of Denmark

GEOGRAPHICAL FEATURE: Zugspitze, the highest mountain in Germany at 9,718 feet (2,962 m)

FOOD: Gummy bears originated here.

OBSCURE FACT: Hike through the Black Forest and you may see lynx, wild boar, or a two-foot-long (0.6 m) earthworm that's unique to the area.

Small Worlds

Miniatur Wunderland

Hamburg Ⓝ 53.5437 Ⓔ 9.9885

Welcome to the world's largest model train setup. But Miniatur Wunderland in Hamburg is so much more. The tracks travel through intricate replicas of Italy, Austria, the United States, and other countries. Each location is packed with astonishing details.

In the miniature Alps, figure skaters whirl and hikers climb the peaks. Tiny people crowd the streets of Wunderland's Hamburg—every square foot has about 23 of them. Las Vegas shines with 30,000 lights. There's even an airport where planes taxi to the runway. Keep your eye out for dramatic moments: police investigating a crime scene, for example, or a polar bear chasing a hapless fisherman around an icy lake.

No matter how carefully you look, you'll never see it all. But some visitors try. Miniatur Wunderland reports that people arrive early in the morning, leave right when the museum closes, and come back the next day for more.

Radioactive Remains

Wunderland Kalkar

Kalkar Ⓝ 51.7629 Ⓔ 6.3256

The fun just radiates from this amusement park. Here you'll ride a roller coaster, relax on a merry-go-round, or go bowling—all on the grounds of a nuclear power plant. You can even take a swing ride inside a huge cooling tower. It's dubbed "Echoland" because your screams will bounce off the giant concrete walls.

Isn't playing in a nuclear plant kind of . . . dangerous? Luckily, this place was never actually radioactive. While the power plant was still being built, the neighbors began to voice their fears about its safety. At one point, 40,000 people took to the streets in protest. So the German government shut the project down.

But then an imaginative Dutch entrepreneur heard about the abandoned reactor and thought, "This would make an *amazing* theme park." And he was right. He bought the place and created Wunderland Kalkar for all to enjoy.

To find a pit of real radioactive waste, grab your Geiger counter and travel 7,833 miles (12,606 km) to a Micronesian island in the western Pacific. That's less than the total distance of Germany's famous highway system, the autobahn—

80

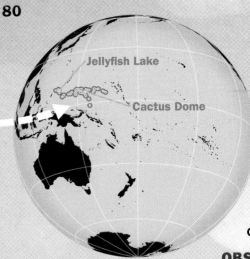

MICRONESIA

LOCATION: western Pacific Ocean

GEOGRAPHY: It's a region consisting of five sovereign states (Federated States of Micronesia, Palau, Kiribati, Marshall Islands, and Nauru) and three US territories.

CAPITAL: Ngerulmud, Palau, is the world's least populous capital of a sovereign country, with 391 people.

OBSCURE FACT: The only land mammals native to Micronesia are bats.

Radioactive Remains

Cactus Dome

Enewetak Atoll, Marshall Islands
Ⓝ 11.5526 Ⓔ 162.3333

In some ways, Enewetak is a tropical paradise. It's an atoll, a chain of lush islands on a ring-shaped coral reef. You can stroll along white sandy beaches or swim in the sea. A few decades ago, though, it was a nightmare. Forty-three nuclear explosions pummeled this place.

From the 1940s to the 1960s, the United States tested nuclear weapons by dropping them on tropical islands. Enewetak was one such site. In fact, the world's first thermonuclear bomb was detonated here. Named Ivy Mike, it was 500 times larger than the one that demolished the Japanese city of Hiroshima.

Over time, Enewetak became dangerously radioactive. So an American military team dug up its toxic soil. They dumped it into a crater made by a bomb named Cactus. Then they sealed it with a 100,000-square-foot (9,290 m²) concrete lid. Called the Cactus Dome, it's a reminder of the destructive force of the United States's nuclear arsenal. Even today, Marshallese people still grapple with the health impacts and devastation caused by those explosions.

Swimming with Friends

Jellyfish Lake

Eil Malk, Palau ⓝ 7.1611 ⓔ 134.3761

In the middle of tiny Eil Malk island in Palau, there's a lake with a secret. Put on your snorkel and diving mask and swim out into the blue-green waters. You'll see a single golden jellyfish pulsing along. Then you'll notice another one. And then a few more. And then, perhaps, *millions of them.* Welcome to Jellyfish Lake.

Why is this lake packed with jellies? Thousands of years ago, melting glaciers caused the sea level to rise around the world. The higher ocean waters washed these animals into the lake, and they've thrived there ever since.

Don't worry: The jellyfish can't harm you. Their stingers are too small to hurt people. Oh, and they're farmers. Inside their bodies are small algae that make sugary food from the sun. The jellyfish eat some of that sugar, and in return, they follow the path of the sun, making sure their algal gardens get plenty of light.

Unfortunately, there have been fewer jellyfish in recent years. Nobody's sure why, but climate change may be to blame: A lack of rainfall could make the lake too salty for jellyfish.

Once you've swum with jellyfish, try paddling with penguins in South Africa. If you swam all the way there, you'd have

SOUTH AFRICA

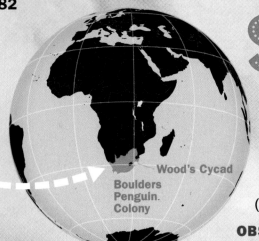

LOCATION: southern tip of Africa

NUMBER OF OFFICIAL LANGUAGES: 11 (the most common first language is Zulu)

OFFICIAL FLOWER: King Protea, with blooms up to 12 inches (304 mm) across

OBSCURE FACT: South Africa has three capitals—Pretoria (the administrative capital), Cape Town (the legislative capital), and Bloemfontein (the judicial capital).

Swimming with Friends

Boulders Penguin Colony

Boulders Beach, Cape Peninsula
ⓢ 34.1957 ⓔ 18.4493

Not all penguins live in Antarctica. Some of them waddle and squawk right near Cape Town, South Africa's second largest city. At Boulders Beach, you can get up close and personal with these tuxedoed birds—and even swim with them!

This sanctuary is the only place where you can observe these endangered African penguins up close. You'll see them preen their feathers, nap on the beach, and feed their fluffy chicks. Oh, and you'll hear them bray— African penguins have a seriously annoying call that sounds like a donkey's "hee-haw."

In the water, though, these birds transform from awkward to elegant. Dive into the sea and you'll see them zip around you at breakneck speed. Just don't touch them. Their beaks are made for snapping up fish, and they're *sharp*.

Tremendous Trees

Wood's Cycad

Ngoya Forest, KwaZulu-Natal Ⓢ 28.8504 Ⓔ 31.6543

You're looking at one of the loneliest plants on Earth.

In 1895, botanist John Medley Wood stumbled across a new kind of cycad—a plant that looks kind of like a palm tree—in South Africa's Ngoya Forest. Excited, he dug it up and planted it in a botanical garden. Soon, researchers went hunting for more of this species, but they couldn't find a single other Wood's cycad.

Cycads can be male or female. The plant that Wood discovered is male. As far as scientists can tell, there aren't any female plants alive anymore. Wood's cycad is doomed to be alone.

Okay, that's not totally true. Cycads can also make clones of themselves. Small offshoots grow on the stem—adorably, they're called pups, and you can detach and plant them. Today, there are a few hundred male Wood's cycads in gardens around the world, including the original here at Durban Botanic Gardens. Perhaps one day scientists will engineer some female partners for these lonesome clones.

In Washington State, you'll find an equally unusual tree. The flights there will take more than 27 hours, so bring plenty of books—maybe some tree field guides?

Vashon
Island
Bike Tree

Mima
Mounds

WASHINGTON STATE

Tremendous Trees

Vashon Island Bike Tree

Vashon Ⓝ 47.4230 Ⓦ 122.4601

On an island in Puget Sound near Seattle, there's a tree that tried to eat a bicycle. Twelve feet up the huge Douglas fir, you'll find a set of handlebars, a front wheel, and half of a rear wheel sticking out of a gnarled trunk.

Why did this tree munch a bike? Nobody knows. The bicycle isn't new—it dates back to the 1950s. According to some people, a kid set it in the fork of the tree and forgot about it. As the fir got bigger, it had no choice but to grow around the metal and rubber. One legend states that the bike is even older—its owner went off to fight in World War I and never returned. Other people think that the whole thing is a hoax. As you stare up at the half-swallowed bike, try to imagine your own spooky story.

LOCATION: the most northwestern state in the contiguous United States

NAME: the only state named after a president (George Washington)

STATE GEM: petrified wood

OBSCURE FACT: You can chew on a wad of gum and stick it to the Gum Wall, a collective art piece in a downtown Seattle alleyway.

Nature's Mysteries
Mima Mounds
Littlerock Ⓝ 46.9053 Ⓦ 123.0475

The landscape of Mima Mounds Natural Area Preserve in southwest Washington seems to have a bit of a skin problem. The vast prairie is covered in mysterious, regularly spaced pimples.

In the mid-1800s, an explorer named Captain Charles Wilkes stumbled across this bumpy prairie. To him, the lumps looked like human burial mounds. But he dug inside one and found nothing but dirt. Since then, all sorts of scientists have tackled the mystery. Some blame vibrations from earthquakes, called seismic activity. The most likely culprit appears to be chubby rodents called pocket gophers. They eat plant roots and push soil from their holes uphill. Each mound may be the work of hundreds of gopher generations.

Or perhaps it's a complicated mix of not one but several factors. It's probably not some kind of geological acne—but if it is, you'd need a few thousand gallons of skin cream to fix it.

Head to NamibRand Nature Reserve in Namibia for another of nature's puzzles. Namibia is more than four times larger than Washington State, but it only has about a third of the population.

NAMIBIA

LOCATION: southwest Africa on the Atlantic Ocean

POPULATION DENSITY: one of the world's lowest, with just 6.7 people per square mile (2.6 per km²)

NAME: after the Namib desert, which means "vast place"

OBSCURE FACT: The largest intact meteorite on the planet sits on a farm near the city of Grootfontein.

Nature's Mysteries

Fairy Circles

Marienfluss Valley Ⓢ **25.0191** Ⓔ **16.0170**

Perfectly round circles of bare soil pockmark the Namibian countryside—and nobody knows why.

Ranging between 7 and 49 feet (2 to 15 m) wide, these bald patches have baffled people the world over. Locals hold that they're the footprints of their supreme god Mukuru. Some people believe they're portals to a fairy realm. Others blame UFOs. To make things even weirder, the spots almost seem to be alive: Over time, they slowly grow and shrink.

Scientists have argued fiercely about the source of these circles. Do they form where plants compete to slurp up scarce water? Or do termites clear these spaces around their nests? Maybe it's a combination of both. Or maybe the fairies here party late into the night, stomping their dance floors bare.

Mind-Blowing Mines

Kolmanskop

Lüderitz, Karas ⓢ **26.7053** ⓔ**15.2297**

Step into a house in the town of Kolmanskop and you won't see any inhabitants. The windows are gone, the paint is peeling, and drifting sand covers the floor. What happened here? In two words: diamond fever.

In 1908, a railway worker was cleaning some tracks and stumbled across a shiny stone. Experts confirmed that it was a diamond. Word spread, and people poured into the region, hoping to strike it rich. They built Kolmanskop with diamond money——a lot of it. In its heyday, the town had a theater, ballroom, casino, hospital, and the first X-ray station south of the equator.

Then the town suffered a double blow. World War I hit, and diamond prices dropped. Plus, people found even larger gems in a different part of Namibia. Kolmanskop was abandoned. Nowadays, the desert is slowly swallowing what's left of the town, making it an eerie—and fascinatingly strange— place to visit.

Want to see a unique working diamond mine? Leave the desert for the frigid lands of northern Canada, 190 miles (306 km) north of Yellowknife. At night, look for northern lights!

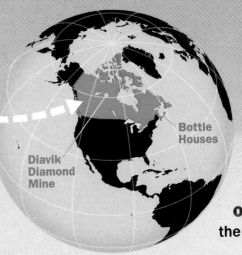

Bottle
Houses

Diavik
Diamond
Mine

CANADA

LOCATION: North America, north of the United States

POPULATION: 36.3 million—fewer people than in California

AREA: 3,855,000 square miles (9,984,663 km²), the world's second largest country

OBSCURE FACT: When a canal freezes in Ottawa, the city clears the ice and you can skate down one of the world's longest rinks.

Mind-Blowing Mines

Diavik Diamond Mine

Lac De Gras Ⓝ 64.4961 Ⓦ 110.6643

Up in Canada's Northwest Territories, you'll find an enormous mine packed with diamonds. It pumps out 3,500 pounds of glittering gems per year. But there's a catch. In the winter, the temperature here regularly drops to −40°F (−40°C) and lower. It's rough on machinery—and people.

Digging up diamonds in the deep cold is hard enough. Shipping them out is a whole other challenge. There aren't any roads nearby. The rugged wilderness is spattered with lakes and marshes that could swallow a heavy, diamond-laden truck.

But the miners have an ingenious strategy. They wait until winter and build an enormous road of ice. Where the ice is too thin, they flood the path with water so it freezes and gets thicker. The road is as wide as a football field, and as trucks roar over it, the ice constantly cracks and refreezes. It lasts for about eight weeks before melting away.

Ultimate Recyclers

Edouard Arsenault Bottle Houses
Wellington, Prince Edward Island Ⓝ 46.4021 Ⓦ 64.1018

In 1979, fisherman and lighthouse keeper Edouard Arsenault received
a set of postcards from his daughter that changed his life. They
depicted a castle made of something unusual: glass bottles. Inspired,
Edouard decided to make his own bottle buildings on Prince Edward
Island. He started collecting containers from local restaurants,
carefully cleaning them and cementing them together to form walls.

Five years and 25,000 bottles later, Edouard had built a house,
a chapel, and a tavern. Tourists flocked to the bottle buildings, and
Edouard became internationally famous.

His creations are marvels of recycling—and they're stunningly
beautiful, too. The glass containers come in all sorts of sizes and
colors. When the sun shines through them, you'll discover their
true beauty: They glow like exquisite stained glass.

You can compare this glass bottle building with a plastic one if you head 5,014 miles (8,069 km) south. It's in
Puerto Iguazú, Argentina, famous for the enormous Iguazú Falls—the world's largest waterfall system.

ARGENTINA

LOCATION: southern South America along the Atlantic Ocean

GEOGRAPHICAL FEATURE: Aconcagua, the highest mountain outside of Asia, at 22,837 feet (6,961 m)

SPORTS: Argentina has the world's most successful World Polo Championships team.

OBSCURE FACT: Cueva de las Manos is a cave containing hundreds of colorful stenciled handprints that date back at least 9,500 years.

Ultimate Recyclers

Ecological Bottle House

Puerto Iguazú, Misiones Ⓢ 25.6248 Ⓦ 54.5543

After you visit this place, you'll never want to throw away another plastic bottle. The Ecological Bottle House in the city of Puerto Iguazú is bright, sunny, and beautiful—and it's made entirely out of trash.

The walls are bottles. The ceiling is lined with juice boxes. The windowpanes and doors are colorful CD cases. Even the furniture is garbage. Because so much of the recycled material is made of clear or colored plastic, sunlight shines through it, filling the rooms with a warm glow.

This extraordinary home is the project of Alfredo Santa Cruz and his family. They're passionate about recycling, and they've taught other people to make bottle houses, too. These dwellings are easy and cheap to build—and they're gentle on the planet.

Ice Caves

Perito Moreno Glacier

Santa Cruz Province Ⓢ 50.4967 Ⓦ 73.1377

Stand next to Perito Moreno Glacier and its sheer size will dazzle you. This blue-white sheet of ice in Argentinian Patagonia is five times bigger than Manhattan, and it's part of an ice field that's the third largest reserve of freshwater in the world. But for a real shock, don't just stand beside it—climb *inside* it.

First you'll need the right equipment. Strap on ice-piercing shoes called crampons, and wear a harness in case you slip. Now you're ready to climb into the caves. Inside, the walls look like polished blue glass. Underground lakes shimmer and rivers gurgle. The tunnels may look sturdy, but don't be fooled. The glacier is constantly flowing, and sometimes parts of it groan, shudder, and even collapse.

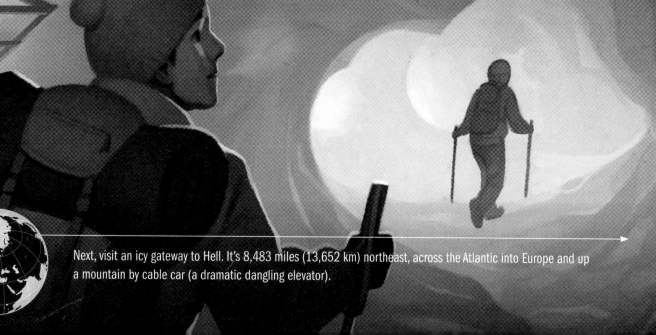

Next, visit an icy gateway to Hell. It's 8,483 miles (13,652 km) northeast, across the Atlantic into Europe and up a mountain by cable car (a dramatic dangling elevator).

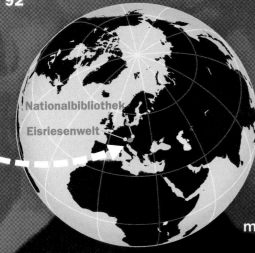

Nationalbibliothek

Eisriesenwelt

AUSTRIA

LOCATION: central Europe, bordered by eight countries

CULTURAL FEATURE: St. Peter Stiftskulinarium, Europe's oldest documented restaurant

LANGUAGE: 88.6 percent of Austrians speak German.

OBSCURE FACT: On a house in Vienna, you'll find a preserved medieval mural of a bespectacled cow and a wolf playing backgammon.

Ice Caves

Eisriesenwelt

Werfen, Salzburg Ⓝ 47.5078 Ⓔ 13.1897

According to Austrian legend, Eisriesenwelt is a gateway to Hell. But it's not fiery hot. This is the planet's largest ice cave—a cavity with ice inside it year-round. Water seeps into it and hits a flow of cold air, creating a frozen wonderland so immense that its name is German for "World of the Ice Giants."

To visit, you'll hop in a cable car and climb up a mountain. The cave opens in the mountainside like a yawning mouth. Step inside and you'll see curtains of icicles hanging from the ceiling. All around you, smooth, icy walls curve and bulge. There are sparkling blue pinnacles like frozen wedding cakes. It's more like paradise than Hell. But you definitely wouldn't want to be stuck inside here alone, or without a lantern to light the way. Who knows what ice giants lurk in the dark?

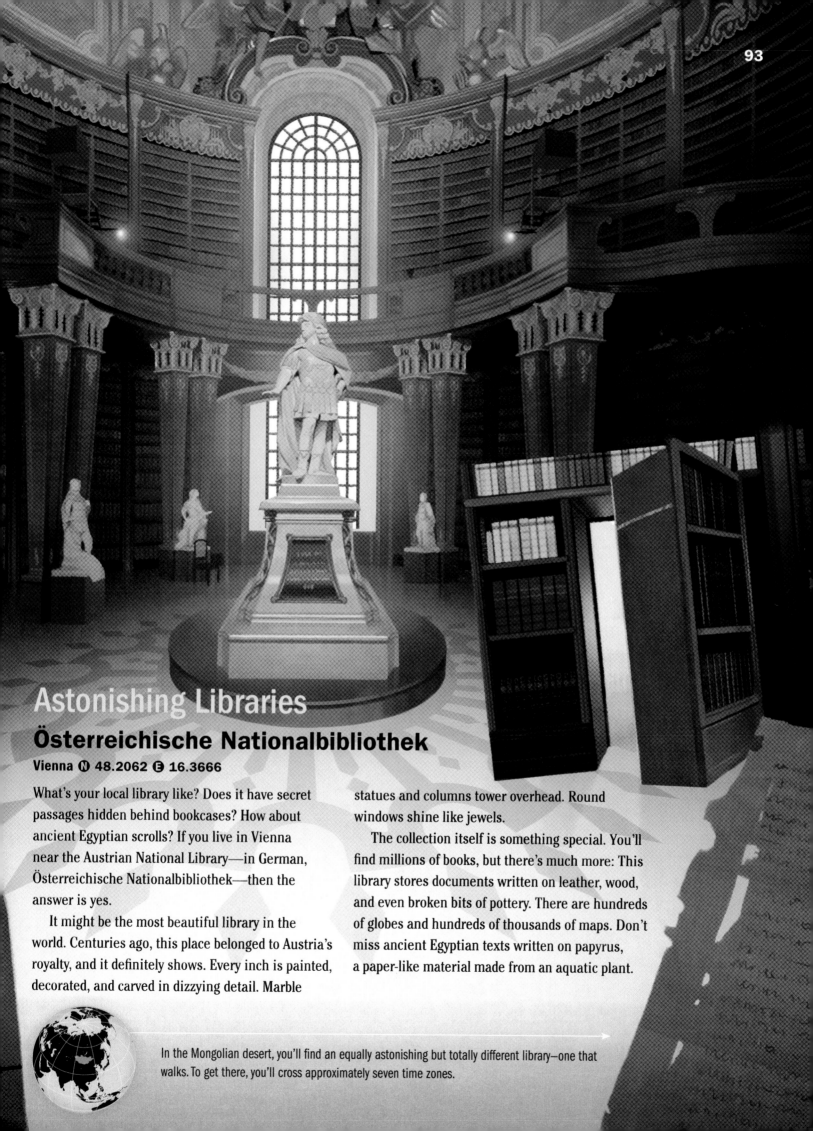

Astonishing Libraries

Österreichische Nationalbibliothek

Vienna Ⓝ 48.2062 Ⓔ 16.3666

What's your local library like? Does it have secret passages hidden behind bookcases? How about ancient Egyptian scrolls? If you live in Vienna near the Austrian National Library—in German, Österreichische Nationalbibliothek—then the answer is yes.

It might be the most beautiful library in the world. Centuries ago, this place belonged to Austria's royalty, and it definitely shows. Every inch is painted, decorated, and carved in dizzying detail. Marble statues and columns tower overhead. Round windows shine like jewels.

The collection itself is something special. You'll find millions of books, but there's much more: This library stores documents written on leather, wood, and even broken bits of pottery. There are hundreds of globes and hundreds of thousands of maps. Don't miss ancient Egyptian texts written on papyrus, a paper-like material made from an aquatic plant.

In the Mongolian desert, you'll find an equally astonishing but totally different library—one that walks. To get there, you'll cross approximately seven time zones.

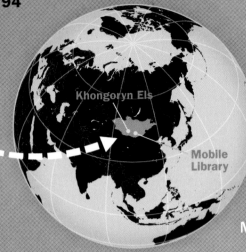

Khongoryn Els

Mobile Library

MONGOLIA

LOCATION: east Asia, north of China and south of Russia

POPULATION: one of the least densely populated countries, with 5 people per square mile

RELIGION: More than half the people are Buddhist.

OBSCURE FACT: The International Intellectual Museum celebrates Mongolia's long history of puzzle-making.

Astonishing Libraries

Children's Mobile Library

Gobi Desert Ⓝ 42.7951 Ⓔ 105.0323

Kids in the remote Mongolian countryside can't easily visit a library. Instead, the library visits them—on the back of a two-humped camel.

This unique project is the creation of children's author Dashdondog Jamba. He's passionate about spreading the love of books to kids who live in isolated places. In 2002, he and a team of volunteers started the Mongolian Children's Mobile Library, carrying a selection of books by camelback across the wide plains and barren deserts.

Why camels? These creatures are brilliantly adapted to Mongolia's environment. Because of their large, spreading toes, they can walk across shifting sands without sinking. Long eyelashes protect their vision during sandstorms. Plus, they carry their own energy stored in fatty humps. Camels may be a little hairier than your average librarian, but they'll never tell you to keep your voice down.

Nature's Music

Khongoryn Els

Gobi Gurvansaikhan National Park Ⓝ 43.7333 Ⓔ 102.3333

In deserts all over the world, you may hear an eerie sound. The sand dunes sing. It's haunting and booming, like a hundred deep-voiced people humming at once.

Singing dunes have enchanted—and terrified—people for centuries. That's true of the Gobi Desert's Khongoryn Els, some of the biggest and most spectacular dunes in Mongolia. The tallest dune is about as tall as the Eiffel Tower. When the conditions are just right, you can hear the sands moan and hum as they fall in avalanches.

Why are some dunes noisy and others silent? There's still a lot we don't know about this phenomenon. Scientists think that size and type of sand grain seem to matter. When the right particles knock into one another, they make tiny sounds. When many of them collide under the right conditions, those voices join together in a roar. The dunes may do more than sing—some even burp.

If the eerie sounds of sand leave you wanting something a little more "rocking," just head west to Azerbaijan. A two-humped (Bactrian) camel can get you there in seven and a half days of riding—stopping to give out books will take a little longer.

AZERBAIJAN

LOCATION: where southwest Asia meets southeast Europe, on the Caspian Sea

FOOD: qutab, savory pancakes filled with veggies or meat

CULTURAL FEATURE: The Museum of Miniature Books includes a tiny Constitution of Azerbaijan.

OBSCURE FACT: About 2,500 people live on Neft Daşlari, the world's first operating offshore oil platform.

Nature's Music

Musical Stone of Gobustan

Gobustan National Park Ⓝ 40.1541 Ⓔ 49.3152

At first glance, the Musical Stone of Gobustan National Park might not seem exciting. It's a beige rock about 6 feet (1.8 m) long. But if you hit it with a smaller stone, you'll hear a lovely, resonant sound. This is the original rock music.

Since ancient times, people may have used this stone to tap out melodies—perhaps for a traditional dance. Look elsewhere in the park and you'll find stone carvings of people prancing in rows, doing something called the *yalli* chain dance. People in Azerbaijan still perform these moves today.

Once you've seen the stone, be sure to explore the rest of Gobustan National Park. It's an alien landscape. Gas vents burn and mud volcanoes bubble, sputter . . . and sometimes explode.

Fiery Wonders

Yanar Dağ

Absheron Peninsula ⓝ 40.5019 Ⓔ 49.8913

At Yanar Dağ you'll sit in a teahouse and sip a hot beverage next to a three-story-tall eternally burning wall of flames. No big deal, right?

Welcome to Azerbaijan, also known as the Land of Fire. When the explorer Marco Polo visited in the thirteenth century, he was shocked to see natural fires burning throughout the region. There's a scientific explanation for the phenomenon: Underground gas reserves leak out at the surface and fuel the flames.

Over time, people have extracted the gas for fuel, causing some of the fires to go out. Yanar Dağ is probably the most impressive one that's still around. It's a stunning sight during the day, but you should really check it out at night. The blaze glows like a neon sign on the pitch-black hillside.

Fired up? Nearby in Turkmenistan, an even hotter sight awaits. To cool down in between, enjoy a breezy ferry service across the Caspian Sea. The Baku-Turkmenbashi service takes just 17 hours.

TURKMENISTAN

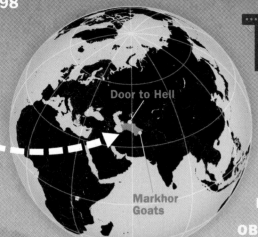

LOCATION: central Asia, north of Iran and Afghanistan and south of Uzbekistan and Kazakhstan

FLAG: features the Islamic crescent moon, five stars, and five complex patterns from the country's traditional carpets

HOLIDAY: national melon festival on the second Sunday of August

OBSCURE FACT: The Akhal-Teke, a symbol of Turkmenistan, is a unique horse breed with a strange metallic sheen to its coat.

Fiery Wonders

Door to Hell

Durweze, Ahal Ⓝ 40.2528 Ⓔ 58.4394

In 1971, Soviet scientists working in a Turkmenistan desert made a big mistake. They accidentally opened a portal to Hell.

The scientists were searching for oil. But they drilled into an unexpectedly large chamber of natural gas—and all hell broke loose. The drilling machinery tumbled into the hole. Dangerous fumes spewed out.

To try and stop the spread of deadly gas, the scientists set the hole on fire, hoping the gas would burn away in a few hours. Forty years later, it's still burning. Oops.

To see the Door to Hell at its best, visit after dark. The crater positively glows in the middle of the black, barren desert. You can stand at the edge, peer down into the flames, and imagine demons dancing the night away.

Gravity-Defying Goats

Markhor Goats

Köýtendag Ⓝ 37.7936 Ⓔ 66.5105

Hike into Köýtendag Nature Reserve and you'll see goats defy gravity. They happily trot across nearly vertical mountainsides and walk along the sheer cliffs of the Pamir-Alay Mountains.

Markhor goats are supremely adapted for climbing. They're compact, with short, powerful legs and wide hooves. Males carry awkwardly huge spiral horns. They use them to battle over females, and that's when their agility really shines: They gallop along the sharp cliffs and smash their heads against each other, somehow without tumbling to their deaths.

Life on Turkmenistan's dizzying cliffs has its advantages. Dangerous predators like lynx and wolves have to move carefully when they're chasing down a Markhor meal. As you watch these goats, don't forget to watch your step!

About 4,247 miles (6,835 km) west in Morocco, you'll see goats go out on a limb. If you saddled up a Markhor goat (not recommended) and it ran at a top speed of 10 mph (16 kph), you'd arrive in just over 17 days of nonstop

MOROCCO

LOCATION: northwest Africa on the Atlantic Ocean

GEOLOGICAL FEATURE: Todra Gorge, one of the world's most spectacular canyons

FOOD: couscous, small balls made of wheat

OBSCURE FACT: The world's longest conveyor belt system carries ore 61 miles (98 km) to the ocean, where boats take it to markets all around the world.

Atlas Studios

Tree Goats

Gravity-Defying Goats

Tree Goats of Morocco

Souss-Massa Ⓝ 30.7000 Ⓦ 9.8333

Walk up to an argan tree on the road between Agadir and Essaouira in southwest Morocco and peer up into the branches. A dozen curious, floppy-eared goats will look back at you. Why did these goats climb the tree? They're looking for some very special fruit.

Argan trees are rare, and to goats, their fruit is totally irresistible. The animals digest the fleshy part of the fruit, but they spit out the seeds. Farmers eagerly scoop up and crush the seeds to make a substance called argan oil. It's sold internationally as an expensive cosmetic product.

This goat-spit economy is both good and bad. Too much harvesting harms argan trees. On the other hand, the money helps Moroccan farmers to send their kids to schools, which are often far away.

Abandoned Film Sets

Atlas Studios

Ouarzazate Ⓝ 30.9335 Ⓦ 6.9370

Take a moment to think about your favorite movies and TV shows. Do any of them have scenes that take place in a desert? If so, they may well have been shot at Atlas Film Studios. Here, the desert is littered with old movie props—some small, and some colossal.

Star Wars. Game of Thrones. The Mummy. These and many more were filmed on this very spot. If you brave the harsh, sand-blown environment, you'll be able to explore the coliseum from the movie *Gladiator*. Turn a corner and you may find yourself on a set that looks like Tibet, Greece, or Egypt.

Sadly, these monuments are all slowly disappearing. Over time, the area's tough climate is wearing them away. So go there soon—and take a video of your trip. That way, you can tell people you starred in a film on a truly legendary set.

Now explore a surprisingly active film set in Malta. It's 1,270 miles (2,044 km) away—about the length of 616 copies of the original *Star Wars* film reel.

MALTA

LOCATION: southern Europe, in the Mediterranean Sea

AREA: 122 square miles (316 km²)—one of the world's smallest countries

GEOGRAPHICAL FEATURE: The Azure Window, a natural stone arch, collapsed into the sea in 2017, and its wreckage is now a dive site.

OBSCURE FACT: Ħal Saflieni Hypogeum, a large tomb, or necropolis, was carved with stone tools and antlers thousands of years ago.

Popeye Village

Mnajdra Temples

Abandoned Film Sets

Popeye Village

Il-Mellieħa, Northern Region

Ⓝ 35.9609 Ⓔ 14.3412

This isn't just a pretty seaside town. You're standing on a 40-year-old movie set. In 1979, a construction crew built an entire village in Malta for a live-action *Popeye* film. They shipped in wood from Canada and the Netherlands, hammered eight tons of nails, and slapped on 2,000 gallons of paint. They even built a breakwater around the village so that rough seas wouldn't interrupt filming.

After the movie was done, the crew departed, leaving the town behind. The locals could have just let it crumble. Instead, they came up with a brilliant plan: They hired their own actors and turned it into a theme park.

Here, you can swim in the bay, play mini golf, hike around, and more. Or, if you don't care about building Popeye-size muscles, just lounge on a sun bed and watch the costumed characters caper by.

Astronomical Archaeology

Mnajdra Temples

Qrendi, Southern Region Ⓝ 35.8267 Ⓔ 14.4365

To really experience the ancient temples at Mnajdra, you need to visit them on one of four special days of the year.

The stone structures perch on the edge of a cliff. Built between 5,600 and 4,500 years ago, they may be older than Stonehenge. One of them has a secret: It was constructed with the path of the sun in mind.

During the annual equinoxes in September and March, when the days and nights are approximately the same length, sunlight pours through the front door and shines down the middle of the chamber. At the two solstices in June and December, when the days are the longest and shortest, the sun lights up special stone structures to the right and to the left.

Archaeologists don't know why the temple was built this way. But they think that Mnajdra was the site of rituals—and even grisly sacrifices.

On a Chilean island that's about half the size of Malta, you'll discover huge statues that catch the sun on the summer solstice. It's an isolated place in the South Pacific, a five-hour flight from mainland Chile.

Ahu Tongariki

Villarrica
Volcano

CHILE

LOCATION: along the southwest coast of South America

AREA: 291,930 square miles (756,095 km²), but it averages just 109 miles (175 km) across

NATIONAL SPORT: rodeo—riders use a traditional horse breed called the Chilean Horse

OBSCURE FACT: The Marble Caves of Chile are a series of natural caverns cut into swirling blue-gray marble that rises from a glacial lake.

Astronomical Archaeology

Ahu Tongariki

Easter Island Ⓢ 27.1258 Ⓦ 109.2769

Visit the island of Rapa Nui on the longest day of the year and you can stand alongside stone giants to watch the sun set into the Pacific.

Rapa Nui, also known as Easter Island, is a lonely place. There aren't any other islands nearby, and mainland Chile is 2,000 miles (3,219 km) away. Yet expert Polynesian sailors landed here and settled down. About 800 years ago, they started to carve stone figures—hundreds of them.

Called *moai*, these statues are gigantic. The largest weighs more than a 737 airplane. They represent ancestors, and they stand between the villages and the sea, protecting the people from the ocean's chaos.

There are several statue-covered stone altars, or *ahu*, on the island. But Ahu Tongariki is special. Its moai are carefully positioned to gaze right into the sinking sun on the summer solstice.

Volcanic Vistas

Caves of the Villarrica Volcano

Pucón, Cautín Ⓢ 39.2667 Ⓦ 72.2167

You'll end your journey the way you started it: by putting on a hard hat and stepping into the heart of a volcano.

As you hike toward Villarrica in southern Chile, you'll see a wisp of smoke rising from the peak. It's a sign that this snow-covered volcano is restless. Villarrica has erupted dozens of times, sometimes with deadly results. After a major eruption in 1971, mudslides and toxic gas killed perhaps dozens of people.

Most of the time, though, it's a peaceful place. And it's riddled with caves that you can safely explore. Inside, you'll see pointy stalactitles and old lava flows that have hardened into solid rock.

Like this volcano, our planet is constantly changing. It's always making new wonders, carving passageways for exciting adventures—some just below your feet.

To return to the place at the start of this book, strike out northeastward over South America and cross the Atlantic to Iceland's Thrihnukagigur Volcano. Though these locations are 7,650 miles (12,311 km) apart and separated

Whew! YOU MADE IT.

CONGRATULATIONS on reaching the end of your around-the-world trip. Grab your favorite snack, find your comfiest chair, and rest your tired feet. You deserve a break.

But are your adventuring days over for good? Nope. In fact, we're going to let you in on another secret . . .

You're just getting started.

On this trip, you glimpsed a tiny fraction of your planet. You traveled to 47 countries out of nearly 200. (Well, that's 193 UN sovereign states, 2 observer states, 6 partial recognition states, 3 more unrecognized de facto states, 45 inhabited dependent territories, and 6 uninhabited territories . . . to be specific!)

The world is teeming with spectacular, obscure places. And that world needs you. It needs young, thoughtful, responsible explorers to visit its wonders, treat them with respect, and help make sure we're taking good care of them.

You may be young, but don't let that stop you. You're capable of incredible things. With a planet this big, you'll need to get started as soon as possible. So eat the last crumbs of your snack, put on some fresh socks, and go explore . . . starting with your own backyard.

We can't wait to see what you'll find.

ALTERNATE ADVENTURE PLANS

Planning your travel route is one of the most fun parts of being an explorer. There are millions of possible paths to take! Interested in plants and animals? You'll go ape over our Fantastic Flora and Fauna route. Love being underground? Try a Subterranean Sojourn. Looking for a spot to plan total global domination? We have you covered with our Super Villain Lair House Tour. Here are a handful of varied routes for the discerning traveler.

METHODS of TRAVEL
by Speed

What's your preferred way to travel? Do you like to sit on a train and watch the world whiz by, or would you rather strike out across the wilderness on horseback? Here are a few travel options you'll find in this book—and how fast they'll get you around. Can you think of some methods we've left out?

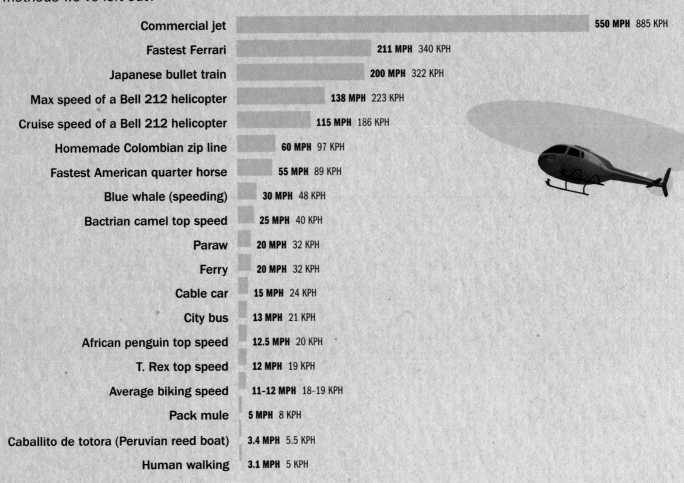

Method	MPH	KPH
Commercial jet	550 MPH	885 KPH
Fastest Ferrari	211 MPH	340 KPH
Japanese bullet train	200 MPH	322 KPH
Max speed of a Bell 212 helicopter	138 MPH	223 KPH
Cruise speed of a Bell 212 helicopter	115 MPH	186 KPH
Homemade Colombian zip line	60 MPH	97 KPH
Fastest American quarter horse	55 MPH	89 KPH
Blue whale (speeding)	30 MPH	48 KPH
Bactrian camel top speed	25 MPH	40 KPH
Paraw	20 MPH	32 KPH
Ferry	20 MPH	32 KPH
Cable car	15 MPH	24 KPH
City bus	13 MPH	21 KPH
African penguin top speed	12.5 MPH	20 KPH
T. Rex top speed	12 MPH	19 KPH
Average biking speed	11-12 MPH	18-19 KPH
Pack mule	5 MPH	8 KPH
Caballito de totora (Peruvian reed boat)	3.4 MPH	5.5 KPH
Human walking	3.1 MPH	5 KPH

LEARN FROM OTHERS

Your travels will be much more meaningful when you do your best to understand what's going on in the place you're visiting. So, it's time to learn. A great way to learn is by asking a fellow kid some questions about themselves. Then, share your own answers. You might ask:

★ What kind of games, hobbies, and sports do you enjoy?

★ What's your school like?

★ Do you have any pets?

★ What's a normal day like for you?

★ Who do you share your home with?

★ Do you have chores? If so, what kind?

★ Do you have a favorite day or holiday of the year?

★ What's your favorite snack?

EXPLORER'S TIPS

You might think that exploring is all about climbing the highest mountain, investigating the deepest cave, or visiting the most countries. It isn't. It's really about a state of mind—a way of approaching the world with curiosity and passion. Every place, including your own house, street, or town, has a unique story to tell you. Here are some tips for unlocking those stories.

ASK QUESTIONS!

★ What's the geology of this place? If you dug down through the soil, what kind of rocks would you find? Do they have fossils? Did streams or oceans tumble these stones? Did powerful volcanoes, shifting tectonic plates, or heavy glaciers change the land?

★ What kind of plants, animals, fungi, and other life-forms can you find? Are there creatures burrowing below your feet? Would you find different animals here depending on the time of day or the season? Which creatures used to live here that are now long gone? Did dinosaurs roam this area, or saber-toothed cats, or wolves?

★ What's the human history of this place? Who was here 10 years ago? 100 years ago? 1,000 years ago? What did people eat back then, and what were their houses like? Did they go to school? What were their struggles? Did settlers from afar colonize this area? If so, who are its indigenous peoples and what do they have to say?

KEEP A RECORD OF INTERESTING PLACES!

Make a list of the things and places that fascinate you. Write down every historical site, unusual shop, or hiking trail that you want to visit. When someone tells you about a place that sounds interesting, add it to your list!

Next, turn these notes into a map. You can buy or print out a map and add your locations. Or, if you're feeling adventurous and artistic, draw your own map. It's one of the all-time best ways to get to know a place.

VISIT!

Choose a spot that you want to explore. See if you can organize a trip with your family, classmates, or friends. When you get there, take notes of the things that you have questions about. Try drawing what you see.

Collect rocks, sand, leaves or flowers (you can dry them in a plant press), or other interesting items. Note: Make sure you're allowed to collect things here! The rules are different depending on where you go. Keep your items in a special bag or box, and record their names and locations. Write down questions you have about those objects.

FOLLOW YOUR INTERESTS!

Curiosity is like a winding, never-ending road, with amazing stops along the way. Once you find a person, place, or thing that really interests you, follow your curiosity. Read as much as you can. Find out if there are museums or libraries dedicated to your specific interest. You might stumble across another topic you're interested in and start following a new road. You might just keep yourself busy for a single happy afternoon. Perhaps you'll discover a lifelong hobby or career path.

Either way, you'll be exploring.

FURTHER READING

A Child Through Time: The Book of Children's History by Catherine Saunders, Sam Priddy, and Katy Lennon
When we study history, we hear a lot about famous rulers and conquerors. But what was life like for ordinary children and families? This book brings that forgotten history to life.

Amazing World Atlas: Bringing the World to Life by Lonely Planet Kids
Dive into this bright and thorough exploration of your world.

Children Just Like Me: A New Celebration of Children Around the World by Phil Wilkinson and Steve Noon
See life through the eyes of kids in 36 countries all around the world.

Dinosaur Empire! (Earth Before Us #1): Journey Through the Mesozoic Era by Abby Howard
This fun, colorful, engaging graphic novel uses up-to-date science to bring the Mesozoic to life!

The Enchanted World by Time-Life Books
A wonderful series of books that chronicle the folklore, myths, and legends of the world.

If the World Were a Village: A Book about the World's People by David J. Smith and Shelagh Armstrong
This book explains fascinating demographic information by representing all of the world's people as a village with just 100 inhabitants.

The Longest Day: Celebrating the Summer Solstice and *The Shortest Day: Celebrating the Winter Solstice* by Wendy Pfeffer
These books discuss the culture and science of the solstices, and include crafts and activities.

Maps by Aleksandra Mizielinska and Daniel Mizielinski
This big, beautiful book of maps has tidbits on culture, wildlife, geographical features, and much more.

The Museum of Lost Wonder by Jeff Hoke
A magical museum in a book. Filled with beautiful illustrations and incredible craft projects, such as building your very own tiny museum.

Mysteries of the Unknown by Time-Life Books
A series of books focused on unusual phenomena—to be read with a critical eye toward their accuracy.

National Audubon Society Guide to Marine Mammals of the World by Brent S. Stewart, Phillip J. Clapham, and James A. Powell
Heading out to sea for some whale watching? This is your essential guide to every species of marine mammal you'll encounter, from big and splashy to small and obscure.

National Geographic Kids Ultimate Dinopedia by Don Lessem and Franco Tempesta
This rich, beautifully illustrated book includes almost every dinosaur ever discovered, and it will turn any kid into a dinomaniac.

Nature Anatomy: The Curious Parts and Pieces of the Natural World by Julia Rothman
Lavishly illustrated, with visual guides to "The Anatomy of a Mushroom" or the "Phases of the Moon," this book turns every backyard, park, and forest into an alien landscape just waiting to be explored.

Not Your Typical Book About the Environment by Elin Kelsey and Clayton Hanmer
It's a rich, deep exploration of environmentalism with a positive spin. You can learn the history of your clothes, game consoles, and other beloved stuff, and discover how everything is connected.

This Is How We Do It: One Day in the Lives of Seven Kids from Around the World by Matt Lamothe
Based on correspondence with real families from across the world, this book is a glimpse into a day in the lives of seven kids.

Trick of the Eye: How Artists Fool Your Brain by Silke Vry
Full of activities and projects, this book introduces you to the many mind-blowing methods that artists use to trick your eyes!

Unbored/Unbored Adventure by Joshua Glenn and Elizabeth Foy
From geocaching to code-cracking, this is a treasure trove of amazing activities and fascinating information. A book that encourages curiosity if ever there was one!

Watcher of the Skies, edited by Rachel Piercey and Emma Wright
Explore space through poetry! Here you'll find astronomy-themed poems of all shapes and sizes, plus prompts to help you write your own.

Atlas Obscura: An Explorer's Guide to the World's Hidden Wonders by Joshua Foer, Dylan Thuras, and Ella Morton
Want more wonder? Ready for a book for grown-ups with a bit more heft? We have 700 of the world's wonders waiting for you!

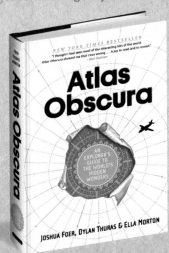